HINTERLAND

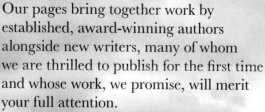

Hinterland offers an answer to the question 'what is creative non-fiction?' by showcasing the best new writing in the fields of memoir, essay, travel and food writing, reportage, psychoscape, biography, flash non-fiction and more.

Our pages bring together work by established, award-winning authors alongside new writers, many of whom we are thrilled to publish for the first time and whose work, we promise, will merit your full attention.

Often, the pieces you'll find in Hinterland will straddle the boundaries between strands and be difficult to classify: we see this as a strength. Hinterland intends to challenge, move, entertain and, above all, be a fantastic read.

WELCOME TO ISSUE 4

Advocates for Hinterland:
Trevor Goul-Wheeker, Nathan Hamilton, Rachel Hore,
Kathryn Hughes, Helen Smith, Rebecca Stott, Ian Thomson

Editorial Team
Editors-In-Chief – Freya Dean & Andrew Kenrick
Art Direction & Design – Tom Hutchings
Business Support – Ben Watkins
Contributing Editor – Yin F. Lim
Editorial Assistant – Charlotte Bishop

Submissions
Hinterland is committed to paying writers and artists for all work we publish.
Please send us your work via Submittable:
hinterlandnonfiction.submittable.com
We accept submissions year-round and endeavour to reply within 4 months.
We regret we are unable to provide feedback.
There is a small fee of £3 per submission.

Subscriptions
An annual subscription to Hinterland
(four issues, print and digital) costs £34 U.K.,
£44 Europe, £54 Rest-of-world.
Digital subscription only, £20.
Please visit our website for full details.

Distribution
Hinterland is distributed worldwide by NBN International.
For all trade orders contact +44 (0) 1752 202301
orders@nbninternational.com

Advertising
Please see our website for current rates, or to discuss sponsorship please
contact us at hinterlandnonfiction@gmail.com

Acknowledgments
The Editors gratefully acknowledge financial contributions from the UEA
Enterprise Santander fund and support from the UEA Publishing Project.

Find Hinterland online at
www.hinterlandnonfiction.com
or contact us: hinterlandnonfiction@gmail.com

ISBN: 978-1-911343-88-2
ISSN (Print): 2632-136X
ISSN (Online): 2632-1378

HINTERLAND

THE BEST NEW CREATIVE NON-FICTION

Issue 4
2020

Issue 4

Editorial

Our submissions pile seemed to explode briefly over the summer months (an indication, perhaps, that writers like to make hay while the sun shines). We were thrilled by this spike and, in particular, the high number of outstanding flash non-fiction pieces we received. To celebrate these bite-sized wonders of writing, we're billing this fourth issue a 'Flash Non-Fiction Special'. It is headed up by a beautifully observed study of the species *Eciton Burchelli*, or army ants, by Mark Cocker; other pieces consider New York City through the decades, the sometimes tragic life of pets, heartbreak, dictators, the wistfulness that can arrive in late-middle age, and Europe's migrant youth.

Elsewhere in this issue: our Ekphrasis feature responds, true to style, to the 40th anniversary of Francis Ford Coppola's *Apocalypse Now*; while places and lives both foreign and familiar are vividly and movingly visited in new writing from John van

Freya Dean is of Dutch-British descent. She graduated from UEA's Creative Writing MA where she received the Lorna Sage award and, the same year, was an Elizabeth Kostova Foundation Finalist. Recent work features in *The Real Story*, *Visual Verse* and UEA's Anthology series.

Kirk, Priya Rajan, Dominic Laing, Rod Panos, Brandon Jackson and Ingrid Fagundez. Cynthia Lewis presents an essay that sits within a new wave of feminist writing: work that responds to past literature and personal experience, interwoven with present-day politics and culture. Our photo essay this issue is by Lily Bungay, lauded 'Rising Star of the Year 2019' and whose work, as you'll see, allows the viewer to step with ease into the frame of other people's lives.

Finally, this issue marks Hinterland's first anniversary. As with all anniversaries, this has prompted a period of reflection on our part (have we done what we set out to? where could we do better?) and an eager anticipation of the year ahead. We'd love to hear your thoughts. What have we got right (or wrong)? What would you like to see in Hinterland's pages in issues to come? Drop us a line, or simply say hello, at: hinterlandnonfiction.com

Andrew Kenrick has worked as an archaeologist and an archivist, a writer and an editor. He is currently studying for a PhD at the University of East Anglia, where he also teaches English Literature and Publishing.

Contributors

Colwill Brown (*Twin Wrecks*) is an instructor and consultant at GrubStreet in Boston and an MFA candidate at the University of Texas at Austin. She is the recipient of the Wellspring House Emerging Writer Fellowship and the Henry Blackwell Essay Prize, and has received fellowships and support from Bread Loaf Writers' Conference, Boston College, Kansas State University, the Anderson Center for Disciplinary Studies, and GrubStreet. Colwill's work is forthcoming in *Granta* magazine.

Lily Bungay (*Deeper than Blue*) is a London-based documentary photographer inspired by nature, close-knit communities and those who live in harmony with the land. Her gentle approach towards her subjects allows stories beneath the surface to arise. With all that she does, Lily aims to shine a light on the beauty that exists within our world. Lily was awarded 'Rising Star of the Year' by *Amateur Photographer* in 2019. Her work has been featured in *The Washington Post* online and BBC News. Lily recently completed an MA in Photojournalism and Documentary Photography. lilybungay.com

Laura Carroll
(*The Riddle of the Sphinx*) is a writer/artist/international development wonk based in the Washington, DC area. She has lived/worked/traveled in 20+ countries and counting. Nearly everything she writes relates to fairy tales in some manner, and she enjoys subtly queering everything she touches. Her previous (non-fiction) work has appeared in *Global Impressions* and *Renaissance Magazine*, as well as various travel writing websites. Most of her fiction and poetry still lives in a drawer.

Mark Cocker (*Dark Sunlight, or My Favourite Predator*) is a naturalist and author of creative non-fiction, who has written for *The Guardian* newspaper for more than 30 years. His 12 books include works of biography, history, literary criticism and memoir. They include *Our Place* (2018) about the fate of British nature in the twentieth century, which was shortlisted for the Thwaites-Wainwright and the Richard Jefferies Prizes. Between them his last four books have been shortlisted for 9 awards. *Crow Country* won the New Angle Prize in 2009 and *A Claxton Diary* won the East Anglian Book Award in 2019.

Ingrid Fagundez (*I Believe*) is a Brazilian writer. She studied Journalism and has worked as a reporter at *Folha de S.Paulo*, the biggest Brazilian newspaper, and for the BBC. She has a MA in Biography and Creative Non-Fiction from the University of East Anglia and currently teaches at Instituto Vera Cruz, a creative writing institute in São Paulo. Her writing focuses on aspects of faith, nature, race and class. Ingrid is working on her first non-fiction book, about the changes within Amazon mythology in light of the rainforest's destruction.

Bairbre Flood (*The Better Life*) is an Irish writer and journalist. Her story *Fejira // to cross* (also set in the Jungle camp in Calais) won first prize in the Fish Memoir Competition 2019. Judge Chrissie Gittins described it as 'a vivid, clear-eyed account which witnesses the facts of these precarious 'blown-apart lives struggling to start again' and makes them plain to see.' @bairbreflood

Melissa Holbrook Pierson (*Memory City*) is the author of five books, including *The Place You Love Is Gone* and *The Perfect Vehicle*. She also co-edited and contributed to the anthology *O.K. You Mugs: Writers on Movie Actors*. She writes from, and sometimes about, the Catskill Mountains of New York, which is where she moved when New York City would no longer have her, or vice versa.

Stacy E. Holden (*Ah Ya Ween [Oh, Where Am I?]*) is an Associate Professor of History at Purdue University, where her research focuses on the modern Middle East and North Africa. She has published scholarly articles on milling in Fez, historic preservation as a colonial policy, the politics of colonial monuments, and a variety of other topics that illuminate everyday life in the Arab world. She is currently writing a travel memoir tracing Edith Wharton's 1917 trip to Morocco as a means of assessing midlife nostalgia. Learn more about her at stacyeholden.com

Tom Hutchings is our in-house graphic designer and photographer, based in the south of London. As a new father, Tom is spending a lot of time trying to remember what sleep is.

Cynthia Lewis (*Who Will Believe Thee?*) is Charles A. Dana Professor of English at Davidson College in North Carolina and has published widely on Shakespeare and his contemporaries, most recently *The game's afoot: A Sports Lover's Introduction to Shakespeare.* Her creative nonfiction has been published in *The Hudson Review*, *New Letters*, *The Antioch Review*, *Southern Cultures*, *The Massachusetts Review* and *Charlotte Magazine*. Four essays have been cited a 'Notable Essay' in the Best American Essays series; *Return Engagement: The Haunting of Hamlet and Dale Earnhardt, Jr.* won Shenandoah's Thomas Carter Essay Prize for 2016; and *Body Doubles* won the Merringoff Prize for nonfiction.

Mia Hague (*Coming Through*) is a full-time illustrator who works from Norwich Artist Studios. Specialising in the medium of collage, she mainly works by hand with paint, found objects, books, maps, and photographs. Her work features original characters and intricate landscapes, with the odd shipping forecast thrown in for good measure. She proudly shows her workings and leaves mistakes in. Mia is open to new collaborations and commissions in 2020 having just launched her new venture, a greetings card business with a difference: www.greylingpost.com.

Molly McCarron (*My Pets*) is a former bookstore clerk, English conversation teacher, equity research analyst and television producer who lives and writes in Toronto. She has written about travel, music, and business in Canadian newspapers and magazines. This is her first published piece of creative non-fiction.

B. W. Jackson (*The Paris Pageant*) is a native of Upstate New York. His fiction has been nominated for a Pushcart Prize.

Tessa McWatt (*In Conversation With…*) is the author of six novels and two books for young people. Her fiction has been nominated for the Governor General's Award, the City of Toronto Book Awards, and the OCM Bocas Prize. She is one of the winners of the Eccles British Library Award 2018 for her first non-fiction book, *Shame On Me: An Anatomy of Race and Belonging.* She co-edited, with Dionne Brand and Rabindranath Maharaj, *Luminous Ink: Writers on Writing in Canada.* She is also a librettist, Professor of Creative Writing at the University of East Anglia, and is on the Board of Trustees at Wasafiri.

Rod Panos (*Chest Wound*) lives in California. A previous life writing reports in pursuit of technical development and corporate goals failed to satisfy his creative urges. The joys of writing now encourage him to write more personal stories hoping to reach a broader audience and of one day pressing the 'submit' button with a bit of confidence.

Priya Rajan (*A Week in Churu and Bikaner*) lives in Bangalore, India. She worked in the software industry for more than a decade and quit for personal priorities. Currently, she is striving to be a writer. Her work has been published in *NatureWriting, Snapdragon, Flock* and *Orion* magazines. Her family is passionate about travelling and they explore the incredible landscapes of India along with their young and adept traveler daughter.

Gerard Sarnat, MD, (*Apocalypse Then and Now*) has won the Poetry in Arts First Place Award and Dorfman Prizes, been nominated for a handful of recent Pushcarts/Best of Net Awards and authored *Homeless Chronicles*, *Disputes*, *17s*, and *Melting The Ice King*. Recent work has appeared in academic journals from Stanford, Oberlin, Wesleyan, Johns Hopkins, Harvard, Pomona, Brown, Columbia, Sichuan, Canberra, University of Chicago; also *Ulster*, *Gargoyle*, *Main Street Rag*, *American Journal Poetry*, *Poetry Quarterly*, *New Delta Review*, *Brooklyn Review*, *LA Review*, *San Francisco Magazine* and *The New York Times*. gerardsarnat.com

Charlie J. Stephens (*Kaleb Blackgoat*) is a queer fiction writer living in Northern California. Charlie has lived all over the U.S. as a bike messenger, wilderness guide, bookseller, and seasonal shark diver (for educational purposes). Charlie's work has appeared in *Original Plumbing* (Feminist Press), *The Flexible Persona*, *The Forge Literary Magazine*, *Gravel Literary Magazine*, *Rappahannock Review*, *Not Your Mother's Breast Milk*, and *Nothing Short of: Selected Tales from 100 Word Story*. Charlie is currently working on a collection of short stories, as well as their first novel. charliejstephenswriting.com

John Van Kirk's (*Pileated in Humboldt Country*) short stories have earned him the O. Henry Award (1993) and The Iowa Review Fiction Prize (2011). His work has been published in numerous journals, as well as several anthologies. His novel, *Song for Chance*, was published in 2013 by Red Hen Press.

HINTERLAND

At Hinterland we are committed to
publishing the best in creative non-fiction
from around the globe.

We are always thrilled to feature work
from established, well-known authors but
have a particular interest in discovering
new voices and in pieces that sit outside
the usual categories: we ask only that
it be a work of non-fiction.

We operate an open, year-round
submissions policy and aim to read
all work submitted within three months.

We pay for all the work that we publish
and receive frequent interest from agents
and publishers regarding our contributors.

Please send us your best work and we
will endeavour to find a place for it.

Guidelines for submissions

- Submissions should be made via Submittable only. Please follow the link below:

- A small fee of £3 per submission applies to non-subscribers. Subscribers enjoy the benefit of submitting their work for free.

- All work should be new, previously unpublished material. If your work is subsequently accepted elsewhere, please kindly let us know.

- Pieces should not run to more than 5000 words. We accept anything from 500 words (very short pieces will be considered for our flash non-fiction slot). We also accept extracts from longer works, or works in progress.

- We warmly embrace writing on any topic, or from any genre, we ask only that it falls somewhere in the realm of non-fiction writing.

- Your work will be considered for all upcoming issues; it might help you to know that we operate a 3-4 month editorial lead time.

- We regret that, due to the number of submissions received, we cannot provide feedback.

hinterland.submittable.com/submit

Ekphrasis

From the Greek ἔκφρασις (ékphrasis), meaning 'description';
a work of art produced as a rhetorical exercise,
in response to another work, real or imagined.

Apocalypse Then and Now

by Gerard Sarnat

'The Horror'

– from Joseph Conrad's book *Heart of Darkness*,
adapted into Francis Ford Coppola's movie *Apocalypse Now*.

i. Admirer Approaches 40th Anniversary of Apocalypse Now

Lifted straight from the pages of Conrad's *Heart of Darkness* and Herzog's *Aguirre, the Wrath of God* cinematography, dropped right out of Coppola's insane Colonel Kurtz/odd Brando lips... my own bad trip, how to get distance or some rest on a bare cot under mosquito netting – this grown boychick squints toward bloody sky at one, maybe more, Apache 'copters' whirring blades to avoid being scalped perhaps sliced into unSolomonic hellish halves by that goddamn overhead fan...

ii. Kadavu Sabbath

Stale chicken soup, wintry morning taste, Sunday dry mouth hangover forty bowls into impossibly hepatitic communal wood basin, all night kava root circle clap-clap ceremony; post grog, groggy on three case stubby beer washdown, running away from myself, I try to keep up with big boys getting down on Cliff and Marley.

Does the gentle terrain explain why this laid-back tropical turquoise paradise's gentle folk evoke Jamaica – minus the stoned green glazed ganja gleams?

Buddhist bardo-brained black happiness painful passageway cauliflower abattoir wet dreams, ankle-deep ash-filled strange gravely sandstorm sounds narrow train track freeways travel through my mind.

Organisms rise sweaty under bug netting waking from cold noisy silence onto laughing waves...

One of three hundred magical Fijian islands, overlooking likely-named Raintree Lake, it pours and pours some more off and on day and night.

A blond lad spends mornings on the deck outside his family's bure. Unhurriedly, time after time, he drops in a corked breakfast-baited line. Sometimes he pulls out little wigglies which I've observed him learn how to de-hook and toss back, waiting for a larger one the lodge has offered to cook. He looks like the serene child moonfishing at the beginning of DreamWorks movies.

Stale chicken soup, wintry morning taste, Sunday dry mouth hangover forty bowls into impossibly hepatitic communal wood basin, all night kava root circle clap-clap ceremony

In the nearby sea, while porpoise dorsal fins play with surfers sunny sailfish peek above whitecaps. Beneath the storm novice scuba divers kiss and worry that hissing raindrops are leaking oxygen lines.

Inside, does the whirring circular ceiling fan turning over hot air signal the beginning of an *Apocalypse Now/Heart of Darkness* nightmarish-insane-Morrison/Conrad This is the End Willard-terminating-Kurtz detritus cycle – a horror-of-it-all upriver hallucination? (Thirty-five years ago on the ocean's other side, in Marin County where Francis lived; dear Aggie, wife to Coppola's editor-supreme Walter Murch and more importantly our midwife; cajoled, Lamazed, and natural childbirthed, then taught us to suckle our first.)

Outside our torrent-pounded thatched roof,

bleached-out blond fatted Mr Wimpy Michelin Man doughboy tourists snorkel and float in remote South Pacific lukewarm amniotic fluid.

Covered head to toe, wary Australians and Kiwis from New Zealand, where an ozone layer hole has created a melanoma epidemic, drip messy suntan and bug lotion.

It wouldn't surprise me if, to local eyes, we self-proclaimed apparent masters of the universe seem lifeless avoidant droids, vamped blood-sucked servants, deluded enslaved worker ants. When electric generators black out (frequently), the phone and computer inside what was an air-conditioned room melt into sweetmeat treats for ravenous red fire ants.

When electric generators black out), the phone and computer inside what was an air-conditioned room melt into sweetmeat treats for red fire ants

… Manual typewriter nursing Chivas on ice boozy Hemingway fantasies …

Boats of vibrant brown curved curly men wearing sperm whale teeth and sounding turtle shell trumpets, lower shark and octopus lures, bamboo crayfish and shrimp traps. Nets knitted from fruit bat bone-needles snare yellow fin tuna in mass scare lines. Razor-toothed barracuda trolls encircle confused gemfish, boxing them in with bubbles, pushing to the surface for the kill. Predatory seabirds rise and fall time after time until finally dive-bombing when the catch arrives at the top. Trawling fishermen come in behind.

Back on shore, roosters crow, palmed parrots talk, mynahs squawk from Captain Bligh's Munity on the Bounty bread trees. Crickets chirp: I try to remember how to derive formulae to calculate the temperature from the speed of hoppers' leg-rubbing. Sunday morning bells chime method-to-their-madness rhyme, calling the natives to Methodist prayer in the nearby village of Naikorokoro.

After peppermint tea, I re-don last night's traditional sulu skirt, scurrying behind Epi, Veranando, Samuel, Seta, my peer elder Alfredi, Thomas, Reverend Alex and the rest of the kava and alcohol-wasted guys. Isaac offers a shortcut in his old-time warrior double-hulled dugout outrigger. Not really old school, appearing like a sharply dressed Eddie Murphy, he drops the religious among us past the coral reef on the village's beach, then quickly excuses himself for more pressing affairs.

Leaving the canoe, learning from recent faux pas, I pause to lift my long skirt. A pig with earrings, feet swollen from bites and anti-bite cream allergies, my ample ankles are my late grandma's thick tree trunks. My wife cautions me to cross my legs in church.

Missionaries eliminated slave-snatching blackbirding from this island about a hundred and thirty years ago. But it is said the evangelists only rid Kadavu of cannibalism around 1964 – when the current chief was already an experienced man.

Native Americans encircle cowboys: the shooter who kills the most Indians gets the girl – or is it the man shooting the most girls who's rewarded with a good-looking Indian? Ladies who think nasty thoughts in their hearts of darkness start growing hair in all sorts of body parts...

In any case, no fool, I hop to the proper amenities too: why take chances they're still a few checkerboard tattooed, scarred ashen five foot-wide hairdo'ed human-flesh scrapie-virus infected warriors insane with Creutzfeldt-Jakob disease, pickling arms and carving sailing needles from human shins, long forks from long bones? Which one might drink kava from my skull, make me watch others eat my body parts, the climax being forced to consume myself before thrown in an oven alive, cooked to humiliate my soul, remove my body's sacred tabu?

Approaching the village, my daughter removes from her shoulders a long, light scarf, which she's worn like a Jewish fringed tallis, and now turns it into a traditional wrap-around sulu skirt. She also wears a Princeton head lantern, which from a distance resembles Jewish tffilin phylacteries.

In 1935 quite a few Polish Jews faithfully fatefully fatally felt the only ones not to be afraid of were the Germans. If only Hitler would come. At least in Germany there's law and order, everyone knows his place. It doesn't matter so much that the mob is terrified of Der Fuhrer. What matters is imposing order. The nightmare scenario, of course, was that one day the priests would say Jesus' blood was flowing again because of the Yids who drink Christian children's blood. That they would start to ring those scary bells; the peasants would pick up their pitchforks. That's the way the butchering always begins.Like when a piglet is killed, it squeals and pleads with that pink-cheeked voice of a tortured child. God sees and hears every creature's grunt, and has no pity on anarchist Antichrists. No body imagined what was really in store. Wealth is a crime, poverty a punishment. Fear and faith are synonyms in Hebrew...

Men dressed in black, red and blue western shirts and jackets and ties with matching traditional Fijian sulu skirts greet us warmly

Corrugated tin-roofed shacks lead to the stone church. Men dressed in black, red and blue western shirts and jackets and ties with matching traditional Fijian sulu skirts greet us warmly. (I think of yesterday at the movies when Fijians howled during *The Hostage*. Something went over our heads, something about Bruce Willis being the chief of police.) The chief comes up to me as our crew's likely elder: we exchange Bula! Bula! greetings, bizarrely reminding me of the totally dissonant beanie-wearing flag-waving Yalies' wailing their Boola! Boola! fight song. Women all in white and pink guide us inside to front row seats of honor.

The Fijian-speaking chieftain, leaning on silk pillows and drapes, leads the service. His presumed in-training son sits next to him: maybe still drunk; he yawns, stares out the window, eventually catches a few zzz's, a kip. We're handed feathered bamboo fans to swat away disjointed long-bodied stinging wasps. The WASPS among us seem to know that numbers 116, 221 and 174 on the wall indicate hymns: they sing along in English with the amazing chorus' four-part Fijian harmony. A trumpeting angel Gabriel hovers.

The village spokesman extends us greetings in English, preaching we're all brothers and sisters before God. Kids in the pew behind me give up their good-natured giggly pinching, get up to pass the collection plate.

If only they knew we were Jews. The Old Testament and Eretz Israel are big-time around here: New Guineans asked my bearded longhaired son whether he was Taliban or descended from Abraham before honoring him…

A few Bula Vinaka thank yous and we're on our way down the oval mountain path, through groves of cassavas, mangoes, guava, cocoanut, orange flame, killer figs, lantana, taro, bougainvillea, avocado. Low tide, we arrive at the sea's crab holes, lobster and kingfisher nests.

An underground oven cannibalizes mahogany wood to fuel a special goodbye lovo feast slow-cooking since dawn. Yesterday we brought produce back from the open market in a huge wheelbarrow. This morning, the kids caught fish from the boat. Isaac put down a pig. It all smells yummy. Before putting unknown meat in my tummy, I ask the old chief man-to-man to assure me that the banana-braided hairy fatty white flesh between the chicken and red snapper is just good old pure unkosher pork – not human.

iii. Upriver

Last night's festivities behind, it's last-chance-for-adventure time before we head back home.

Wolfing down blood oranges and poached eggs with the family, I head out alone, east along the northern shore. Kadavu musk-parrots shriek 'KANDAVU!' – probably the reason natives add an 'n' when pronouncing the island's name. Marveling over exquisitely spiraled yellow, pink and white scallops, conches, whelks and starfish; the world is my oyster.

I follow the creek inland. About a hundred yards upstream, zany Dr Seuss-ish skipper fish, heads up like alert water skiers, skim the surface on their tails. Another fifty Darwinian yards inland, they've increased from small guppies to medium trout. A turtle's head bobs up from its shell like Captain Nemo's periscope. *Twenty Thousand Leagues Under the Sea* was one of my favorite kids' movies. Exquisite slithery slivery fluorescent geckos and red smushy newts slide underfoot.

Sand gives way to rock as I ascend south-east. The lush green canopy shelters the cut-glass crystal-clear blue lagoon from the rain. Black and white millipedes inch along the ground. Monarchs surge overhead, reflexively triggering my humming, 'Zippity do dah, Zippity eah. My oh my what a wonderful day...' I flashback to childhood memories of the amazing butterflies in the animated feature film Uncle Remus.

Leaving the rainforest's cover, it's drizzling pleasantly. Slipping on the sharp boulders, I break off a sturdy tree branch to better support cartilage-less knees. My internal soundtrack flips to Doc in *Snow White and the Seven Dwarfs*, 'Hi ho, hi ho, it's off to work we go.' It's a regular Disney moment out here.

I ... see raggedy filthy shorts, a broad tattooed chest, a tangle of disheveled hair on a young man with nose bones holding a wood pitchfork

Thud! My glasses and I fall. Although body parts seem no worse off than before, a palm and elbow sting and drip blood. Like Piggy in Lord of the Flies, I fumble around for my glasses. Luckily, my searching fingers find them unbroken. Reaching over, I'm startled by two bare brown feet a foot in front of me. Looking up, I gradually see raggedy filthy shorts, a broad tattooed chest, a tangle of disheveled hair on a young man with nose bones holding a wood pitchfork with three sharp metal blades. This guy looks just like the hundred-plus year-old cannibal photos in the museum. What's going on? Who is this dude?

Be real, Ger, no time to panic, learn from past mistakes when you've overreacted. Within a millisecond, my spinning mind retreats into a flood of loony-in-retrospect family jokes I'm the butt of, stories I'm constantly kidded about.

On safari in Kenya, a horde of tall thin red-robed spear-bearing blue-black Masai tribesmen wade across a river toward us: I yell for my wife and two small kids to get behind me, I'll protect you; the warriors cross over... smiling, sheepishly offering to sell trinkets, trade a spear for Eli's camera.

Stripping to undies, jumping into the Pacific to rescue a capsized middle-aged lady...who turned out to be a most ungrateful master kayaker.

In Belize, the brute jumping out from nowhere toward my younger daughter, three hours into what felt like a forced-march through torrential mud looking for Indian ruins... to give her an umbrella.

Alone with my older daughter deep in northwest Thailand's rice paddies, hours after leaving the Lanu Red's village, a man runs at her wielding what looked like a club...a generous, if blottoed, Lanu White extending us his opium pipe, inviting us – Come Over to My House, Come Over to Play – to stare at a receptionless blank TV screen.

So, cool it, man. I gather myself, rise to stand tall (all five feet five inches of me), and summon a hearty Bula! Bula! Unlike every other Fijian, who's out-smiled and out-Bula Naka'd me back, this fellow just stares, suspicious, clearly not happy to see me, arms on spear, holding his ground, not moving on. I hold my walking stick firmly in front of me.

Although last night I'd dismissed Susan's news as so much gossip, I reconsider. The owner of the adjacent resort recently fell to his death from a cliff. He catered to the high-end $3000-a-night likes of Madonna, offering cement-bunker security and isolation instead of our up-close-and-personal bourgeois experience. Rumors have it that he abused the Fijian staff, which may have had something to do with his accident.

Now I'm totally focused, no yucks or campy drama-king inner giggles about what a cool story this will make. I pause to look briefly into his ghostly eyes. Then, careful not to touch, I slowly walk around him as calmly and confidently as I can muster. Not looking back, I proceed up toward the suddenly threatening misty peaks. From nowhere, a gibberish of Wounded Knee, Slippery Rock, and Captain Ahab jangle my head. Good job, Sarnat, no point fooling around if there's any possibility he didn't understand or wouldn't be deterred by the international ramifications, the big hurt that would descend if he ate an American.

Not hearing rustling or steps behind me, the self-recriminations and second-guessing start. My god, what if you've violated his tribe's territorial boundary? You idiot, he was just as shocked as you, he's probably hightailing it back to the village where you attended church yesterday. You wimp!

Nevertheless, relieved to be safe, my adrenalized fight-or-flight rush turns romantic, into a Wordsworthian Intimations of Immortality natural high. A half-eaten honeycomb and an intact tiny blue egg generate sublime epiphanies. I go forward. The ecstasy proves short-lived.

Way too full of myself, not concentrating on my next step, I collapse into a mud hole. Skittish, crookedly black crabs scoot from their holes under my feet. Delusions of grandeur instantly shift back to dread. Pulling myself up, tubers become snakes entwining my ankles. Twigs become giant walking stick insects that snatch at me. Low-slung gnarly black-hooped mangrove trellises, strangely rooted in the sand at both ends, come alive to entangle me in the nasties. My sweat and blood attract every kind of bug. Sheets of rain bite into my skin. I retreat under a tree – until I smell lightening char. The rocks are impossibly slick. The path is sometimes underwater, sometimes washed out.

> **Tubers become snakes entwining my ankles. Twigs become giant walking stick insects that snatch at me. Low-slung gnarly black-hooped mangrove trellises ... entangle me in the nasties**

With that, I'm done. No trouble convincing myself that I've got a good excuse for the family, that after two hours in the elements, they're all worrying about my whereabouts. We've got a plane to catch. Time to turn around, retrace my steps..

He's nowhere in sight as I return to the point of our brief encounter. The storm rat-a-tats the now black lagoon like a machine gun. A black and tan water snake – the tan camouflaged by the sandy bottom making it look like a string of undulating black diamonds – swims toward my open sandal. Making it back to the open-spaced beach, I stumble on sharp shells, cutting my big toe…

Now showered and comfy, I wonder what the hell actually happened.

I'll bet if the kids had been in my shoes, they'd have made friends and invited him back. Right now, they'd be enjoying tea together… Although sympathetic, my family obviously doesn't know what to make of my story. In any case, enough is enough for me at sixty. Back in time for a quick nap and snack. Before lunch, I pull Papagena's Canadian manager aside. 'Don, I have no idea what really occurred, but you should know about it. I'd appreciate your being discrete if you make inquiries...'

He's the only person who eats at both the staff and the guest tables. 'My little white man, I heard you had a scare today'

Don said he'd never heard another like this, that all tourist-Fijian meetings have been friendly. 'Every once in a while, the villagers chase off a hunter spotted poaching game on Naikorokoro land, but it's never happened on the resort side.'After lunch, Mele comes over, formally but sheepishly. 'I apologize to you and your family.' That was all. He left without further explanation.

Then Samson sidles over, putting his arm around me. A huge affable brown New Zealand Maori who's been the divemaster here for six years, he often serves an intermediary role between the Fijians and the Westerners. He's the only person who eats at both the staff and the guest tables. 'My little white man, I heard you had a scare today. You encountered Mele's brother. He's the village idiot, an idler, no good. Never works, a longhaired hippy. He was sneaking off to spearfish in the ocean when you came upon him. At times he gets stoned into oblivion, so bad he can barely talk or walk. But you needn't worry, he's meek and mild and wouldn't hurt a fly.' All remnants of a Kurtzian mystery dispelled, I join the family on the Nunu Moi to motorboat to the local airport, then puddle jump to Nadi before jetting home into our routine California lives. But before we hop on, our hosts, the sweetest people in the world, place leis around our necks and hold us around our waists as we sing our last four-part harmonies together. Kisses and hugs, then we jump on board, wave, and toss our flowers back toward shore, leaving our hearts in Kadavu, our intention to return.

Au sa liu mada, see you later, not goodbye. ◼

FLASH NON-FICTION SPECIAL

To celebrate Hinterland's first anniversary issue, and in recognition of the wonderful bite-sized non-fiction that appears each month in our reading pile, we're thrilled to present this Flash Non-Fiction Special: 32 pages of the best short-form pieces around.

Mark Cocker leads with an homage to the species *Eciton Burchelli*, the army ant; while others delve into subjects as diverse as migrant camps, New York City, inter-racial relationships, the joy and pain of keeping pets, the fall of dictators, and heartbreak. Enjoy.

Dark Sunlight, or, My Favourite Predator

Mark Cocker

What's your favourite predator? Not a question you hear much nowadays, but the game was grist to the mill in our school playground. I can easily recall myself captured by the meaningless exercise, and giving it the full force of my complete ignorance. In those days I'd barely seen a fox sidle up to a dustbin, let alone encountered real predators. But I can tell you that I was six when I met the creature I now consider to be my favourite. It came about because of a children's book: *The Wonders of Life on Earth*.

Published in 1963, *The Wonders of Life on Earth* was ahead of its competition with state-of-the-art action photography and some rather wonderful paintings. These were a series of fold-out panoramas each focused on an important habitat: rainforest, African savannah, the sea-weathered lava shores of the Galapagos, the montane forests of New Guinea. Into these tableaux the various artists had introduced as many animals as could possibly be fitted onto the page. The results were wildly improbable, luridly vibrant, promiscuously jumbled and about as affecting to a child's imagination as anything I'd seen. In some ways it still is: I have that book 54 years later. To me, at six years old, the additional third folio – which had to be unfurled manually – made it seem as if the life depicted on those pages were spilling out into the real world.

The most affecting was a linked triptych on each side of the three-page spread, by a man called Rudolf Freund. The first was deeply macabre and more intensely packed with organisms even by the standards of this extraordinary book. Most of the animals were ants in their thousands and even tens of thousands (how on Earth, one now wonders, did Freund conceive of such a painting, let alone execute it?). Ants writhing over other ants, ants attacking spiders, smothering tarantulas. Ants everywhere, pouring across the forest floor in sinuous choking masses onto flowers, fungi, leaves, trouping up twigs and branches. Ants on wasp nests even, or clustered together in an immense fermenting mass like an ant swamp.

The first moment that I encountered that arresting triptych in the flesh, I was in Ecuador; the year 1995. As a callow birder I was obsessed with the teeming avifauna for which the Neotropical rainforest is famous. The Amazon holds more bird diversity than any other region on Earth and yet no place seemed more unwilling to let me enjoy its fantastical flocks – the tinamous, hoatzins, trogons, toucans, macaws, amazons, attilas and pihas.

It is a thing television doesn't tell you about the rainforest: the sheer neck strain from looking constantly upwards, fifty metres into the canopy. The sun dazzle that turns all birds overhead into featureless silhouettes; the darkness on the forest floor that makes everything below a mere shadow; and all that you do see well so often fragmented by an enveloping curtain of leaves or vines.

In a rush to explain its ecological complexity, few mention the claustrophobia and enervating heat of the rainforest. Your own body is a key source of major distress – the sweat that leaves clothes soaked and clinging and sets up, in turn, an unfortunate, never-quite-dispersing condensation on both spectacles and binoculars, which means everything is seen dimly, as if viewed underwater. After days of the same steaming conditions, you embrace them as a sort of moral extra to all the aesthetic pleasure of the natural history. Of Neotropical birding, a friend once said, 'I feel as if the sweat and heat and discomfort are good for me, in the way that purgatory prepares you for heaven.'

This was the background to my encounter with army ants. Because, as I looked up, straining to catch sight of birds overhead, I was oblivious to insects coming to meet me across the forest floor. The first I knew of it was intense pain erupting at my shoulder, in the hollow at the back of the knee, in the fleshy part of the neck and, most bizarre, inside the elasticated band to my underpants. The sting of these insects is so discomfiting that it robs you of any decency. Many times I have seen grown men hopping around a rainforest with trousers round their ankles in a state of darkly comic anxiety, while they remove unseen predators from various bits of their lower body.

You discover that a big worker ant has such a hard chitinous exterior that a slap or brush of the human hand is seldom enough to dislodge it, let alone kill it. And death seldom deters it from its mission. Liberated from a body, the ant's jaws maintain the same vice-like grip they held in life. It is for this reason that Amerindians, if they have a flesh wound, are said to seize these minute soldiers, have the insect bite them across a cut, then nip out the abdomen, leaving the creature's head and lock-jawed pincers closing the wound like a medical suture.

My first true observation of army ants came once I'd learnt to maintain proper surveillance of the ground at my feet. Unlike other members of the large *Formicidae* family, many army ants have no permanent subterranean nest. Most are nomads that forage perpetually across the forest surface. Intermittently, however, they gather at a temporary bivouac, a three-dimensional cylindrical cluster. In *The Wonders of Life on Earth*, it was this that looked to me like an ant swamp. The fermenting mass on the page was, in truth, comprised of ant bodies, because the insects are both the architects of a bivouac and its architecture. The workers knit together, leg-to-leg, in a massive, self-heating chitinous weave that is resistant to the effects of weather; and at whose protective heart is the colony's queen with her precious brood of eggs and larval young.

Locating a full bivouac is rare, but what I have found are fragments; foraging columns, caught perhaps by the fall of night and unable to return to the colony proper. These outlying commandos lock together bodily in exactly the same way; in the dim conditions of morning, they resemble nothing more than a strange reddish-brown stick, or tree-root threaded for metres through the forest floor. I would crouch and touch them with a twig. Instantly the thing atomised into a thousand furious parts. With those strategic centimetres between us, I could savour the mechanics of an angry swarm, the way their long, articulated antennae waved and sampled my personal chemistry, how the long coal-tongue jaws advanced blindly.

Relative size is undoubtedly part of the disproportionate impact of an ant swarm. I'll try to explain. Just a single soldier, mounting your leg, pincers waving, is enough to cause concern in a human observer. Multiply that a hundred times and it induces genuine anxiety. But see them seethe across a forest floor in hundreds of thousands, possibly millions – as I did in Panama in the Soberania National Park on one unforgettable morning – and you feel a sense of electric excitement. As you watch, it is intriguing to compute that each insect weighs 1-5 micrograms. Your fear is generated by a creature that is perhaps one-millionth of your own weight.

In any hunting ant swarm there are two interlocking arthropod groups, just as the event provokes a dual emotional reaction. For, as the ants advance like dark spreading sunlight across a fan-shaped arc of roughly 15 metres, so their potential victims flee in a shadow delta of anxiety. Amid all the insidiously soft susurration of formicine legs and bodies bristling across the forest floor, you can hear the 'plop' and 'thump' of crickets and other jumping insects making an escape. Look closer and you can see a tide of refugees: spiders, millipedes, cockroaches, beetles and every creeping thing that ants eat. It is hard not to project on to these lowly creatures some part of the terror that you would feel if similarly assaulted. At the same time you can't resist a sense of horror-tinged fascination at the ants' inexorable progress.

Anything that is slower than the ant's pace of roughly 30 centimetres a minute is assaulted. The pioneers of the raid are fearsome individuals known as 'majors', possessing disproportionately enormous jaws shaped like a pair of scimitars. With these foremost they harry, bite, assassinate and dismember all in their path. Meanwhile lesser workers – known as 'minors' – cut up, process and ferry back to the bivouac the fresh booty secured at the front. The main prey for an ant such as *Eciton burchelli*, which comprised the swarm I saw at Soberania, are other ant species and their brood, of which there can be over 7 million in any hectare of rainforest. They also take fellow members of their own insect order the Hymenoptera, which was presumably why Rudolf Freund depicts ants enveloping a wasps' nest in *The Wonders of Life on Earth*.

The entire range of army ants' victims is a matter of glorious speculation. What has been recorded is remarkable enough. Eciton burchelli lacks the necessary cutting jaws to tackle many vertebrates, but they can and do despatch scorpions, lizards, snakes and baby birds. In 1959 a Jesuit priest reported driver ants in West Africa that killed 10 chickens, 5-6 rabbits and a sheep. It is said that a tethered cow can be polished off in a matter of hours. I recall vividly, in Benin, how villagers reported the frequent loss of chickens but – as long as they were properly prepared – tolerated visits from safari ants because they rid their homes of all other pests. Two choice, if admittedly uncorroborated stories, that I prize for the way they subvert our stock notions of this top predator, involve ants killing crocodiles and lions. The latter was apparently a male held in Brazzaville zoo where, unable to escape, it was reduced to little more than a skeleton.

There is a further, important dimension to this relentless killing machinery that I must highlight in choosing *Eciton burchelli* as my favourite predator. It hinges on the fact that the entire column is one family; a formidable sisterhood frequently laying down their lives for one another. It is this familial devotion and collaboration which makes ant swarms so unassailable. Largely blind and unable to hear airborne sound, the ants are obedient to a set of pheromone signals. It is this ferment of female ant chemistry that gives the hunting swarm its musky odour. Equally the flow of victims ferried to the bivouac – an average raid nets 30,000 items – is itself an expression of the same shared enterprise: the spoils are nourishment for a new generations of sisters. The entire hunting mission is triggered by a mother who, in a single burst of astonishing fecundity, has given birth to between 100,000 and 300,000 offspring.

My sense of awe is compounded by the fact that scientists now know army-ant taxonomy involves two major but separate lineages. The one in tropical Africa culminates in the ants of the genus *Dorylus*, which have given rise to what is probably the largest formicine spectacle on Earth. Some colonies number 25 million workers and over her entire life a queen Dorylus ant can bear 300 million offspring. In Central and South America the same niche is occupied by about 150 species of swarm-raiding ant. Mature colonies among this group achieve more modest figures (1-2 million individuals in the case of *Eciton burchelli*). But the common ancestor that gave rise to the two separate branches pre-dated the separation of Africa from South America, and must have evolved sometime during the early-Cretaceous, at least 110 million years ago. It means that when you are confronted with that incessant flux of dark sunlight, you may recall amid a ferment of instantaneous reactions that you are witness to a predator as old as the Atlantic Ocean. ◧

My Pets

Molly McCarron

One of the earliest books I wrote as a child is called
'My Pets'. It's a small book – we had been making
them in class that way, I think – a page of eight and
a half by eleven paper, landscape style, folded in
half on the short edge and then stapled at one side.

On the first side of each page a pet is introduced.
There are a surprising number of them, maybe
four or five; my handwriting suggests I had not
yet completed the printing drills of first grade. The
front of each page names the pet, for example, 'This
is my cat, Ruby Tuesday.' There is a drawing; the
pet looks happy, there is the obligatory sun shining
out of one corner, the occasional flower or tree in
the background.

On the back side of each page, the hammer drops.
This is my cat, Ruby Tuesday. She ran away.
(Perhaps it was a poor choice of name.)
This is my dog, Max. We gave him away.
(Replaced by a new brother.)
This is my hamster. It got loose.
(And disappeared.)

There are more. The pages recording the losses are
dotted with tears and rain and sad faces – high drama.

I don't remember drawing this book. I found it in
a box in my basement, one of many early illustrated
oeuvres, and while I started mostly with these fact-
based stories, I quickly moved onto fiction.

My husband read it, looked back at the front of it, and asked me how old I'd been when I wrote it. I estimated five or six.

'That's a lot of loss,' he said.

But those losses are so early, they're not even the ones I remember. Beloved Shep, the neighbour's dog. Flopsy, the rabbit who died within a week of adoption into our house, quickly replaced by Thunder, who lived for an endless decade. Sammy, the dog after Max, who was disappeared, our whole block believed, by the writers next door, who always complained about the puppy's noise.

And then there are the mysteries, the few exits my parents did shield me from. A few years ago, I was driving somewhere with my mother, and we got to talking about the menagerie of pets I'd grown up with.

'Oh, but the worst was when one of the pet rats ate the other,' shuddered my mother. I froze. Rose and Violet? My understanding had been that one had died and the other adorable, lovable white hooded rat was so sad that we needed to give it back to the pet store. The worst thing they did that I'd been aware of was nibbling at anything near their cage, so that for years afterward our plastic juice cups were lined with a row of decorative bite marks at the top.

There was another loss not on the page. My mother had a baby when I was about two, who lived for a day after it was born, always known, whenever spoken about later, as 'the baby that died.' Did I sense that? – a toddler watching her mother grow bigger, excited and scared by the promise of a sibling, watching then the sorrow and confusion that resulted?

Did that make me especially attuned to loss?

There was one cat we had for a long time, or a long time by our family's standards. Willoughby was the gentlest and fluffiest cat, submitting uncomplainingly to dress-up and acrobatics orchestrated by my younger brother and sister. I had been away at university when Willoughby died, and I'd always assumed she'd died of old age. Recently, in another review of pets we-have-known, this time with my sister, I asked how it had happened.

'You don't remember? It was awful. She was killed by dogs in the alleyway.' My sister had heard the whole thing, and by the time she'd found my mother to confront the dogs, sweet Willoughby had died.

I don't own any pets. ▪

Twin Wrecks

Colwill Brown

I knew it was over. We say it to each other over tequila cocktails, over notebooks and bagels on writing days, over the desk partition in the office where we first met. *I knew it was over when she didn't care I got this job, when she started texting that other dude, when she said how much she liked 'Soldier' by Destiny's Child.* That's you. And me: *I knew it was over when he got drunk at my boss's wedding shower, when he voted for Romney, when he voted for McCain.*

This is the refrain of our new partnership, which is stitched together from the rags of two others. 'I need a Soldier', you'll repeat. 'How about, I need a dude with a college education'. I'll nod and stroke your hair. 'They kicked him out of the place', I'll follow. 'I found him passed out on the toilet'. We'll dip long-handled spoons into the same sundae and hold hands under the table.

When she told me to stop wearing turtlenecks and I went out and bought one immediately. When I thought I was pregnant and considered having an abortion without telling him. When she needed to mourn the fact that she wasn't marrying a Korean man. When I kissed the Polish boy at my boss's wedding shower. When she resented my lack of social status. When he told me my pubic hair turned his stomach.

One evening, too many tequila cocktails sour the
consolations we pass between us, and I Uber to my
side of the river, to sleep in my own bed. My driver
is Caribbean, born on Saint Thomas. We talk about
the business of belonging to elsewheres.

    'What brought you here,' I ask.

    'My sister, man. She convinced me.'

    'Everybody moves here for somebody else', I say.

    He nods and finds my eyes in the rearview.

    'Too true,' he says. 'Too true.'

Before we were ours, we were somebody else's,
each of us tangled in the laundry of their desires,
bashing around in a washing machine stuffed with
babies and Roth IRAs. And, on finding ourselves
wrung out and hung, we discovered we'd each
packed a U-Haul in our separate Midwestern cities
and relocated to someone else's life, in separate
apartments on the outskirts of Boston.

    I imagine us in those apartments as twin wrecks,
two pairs of vehicles spinning synchronically out of
control on adjacent streets, atomized glass sparkling
across blacktop.

    And after the wrecks, we dusted ourselves off in a
city we'd each moved to for someone else, salvaging
what we could and clinging to our brand-new office
desks, to the open face peering back at us over
the partition.

    Why do we live here? We ask it over the raw honey
and rock salt so carefully arranged on the Sunday
breakfast table, over our naked bodies twisted up
together at two a.m., over escape plans scrawled in

the back of notebooks on should-be-writing days.
It is our middle eight, the switch in rhythm and
pulse between the twelve-bar blues, the steady beat
of *I knew*. ∎

The Riddle of the Sphinx

Laura Carroll

Monsters exist, at the edges of the world. Some monsters will kill you outright, or imprison you, or transform you into your basest animal self. Others will ask awkward questions, with the surety that warriors and travelers are not often philosophers and their answers will be entertainingly incorrect. For any cat-like creature, toying with prey brings half the joy.

Wily Odysseus, returning home from the Trojan War, famously solved the Sphinx's riddle. For someone so clever and cunning, being a warrior and philosopher and traveler were not elements at odds.

My fiancée, on the phone, the night before I went to see the Pyramids of Giza: If the Sphinx asks you a riddle, the answer is Man.

Habibti, I answered, she doesn't talk to tourists anymore. And anyways, I'm sure that her riddle has changed at some point in the last few thousand years.

Doesn't matter, she told me. The answer is still Man.

The year is 2011 and the southern and eastern coasts of the Mediterranean have erupted in revolution. In Egypt, Mubarak has been deposed and the leadership of the country has been transferred to the Supreme Council of the Armed Forces (SCAF).

In the early days, the heady days of revolutionary aftermath, idealism ran high and everyone was a family. United. Freedom, *al-hourayya*, was the word on everyone's lips. Every Friday, whole families came to Tahrir Square after mosque, and there was music and happiness, a festival atmosphere, with balloons and knickknacks and street food for sale. So my friends tell me, the ones who were there.

I never went. I wasn't in Egypt at the beginning of the revolution, and it wasn't safe for me to be there by the end. By the time I arrived in September, the original hopefulness of the revolution was still present, but worn. Friday's festival atmosphere persisted until sundown, developing overnight, and into Saturday, towards protest; the kind of protest that brought down Mubarak, and which now tried to bring down SCAF. Al-hourayya was still the word on everyone's lips, but their lips also tasted tear gas and their bodies felt the sting of rubber bullets.

I gave my Egyptian friends money to buy gas masks and first aid kits. But I'd seen the videos of women protesters being sexually assaulted in the square. I'd seen footage of the raids on NGO offices, the seizure of computers and documents. Three American students were arrested for attending a protest, then deported on charges of espionage. Following the deportation, the U.S. Embassy in Cairo sent an email to all registered expats. The words were fancy but the message was simple: If you do something stupid and get yourself arrested, we really can't help you. Don't do anything dumb.

I was in Egypt for academic research, under the auspices of a tiny international NGO. My appearance was unequivocally foreign, and my Arabic was abysmal despite my best efforts. I'd have lasted for maybe fifteen minutes if I went to Tahrir.

My Egyptian friends made a joke of this. *Sabah-al khayr*, ya-Laura, you haven't been arrested yet?

Shut up! I'd respond, every time. I didn't have a better reply. Expats were leaving the country in droves, and my family back home called every few days asking whether I was ready to leave. Was finishing my master's thesis really worth hanging around the festering remains of a revolution?

I could see the writing on the wall as clearly as anyone else, even if I couldn't read the Arabic script. This revolution wasn't getting any closer to the immediate freedom that its instigators dreamed of, and suspicion and infighting were breaking up the unity that had characterized the early days, when everyone was everyone else's brother.

Protests in Tahrir became larger, and police responses became more violent. SCAF ruled the country despite massed opposition, and no one trusted the upcoming elections that would determine the next president. With the main choice between a former member of Mubarak's government and a leader of the Muslim Brotherhood, it felt like a deal with a devil either way. And the new constitution? No one was sure that there would even be one, let alone what it might say.

There were rumors of live ammunition among the rubber bullet shots. It was said that an officer nicknamed 'the eye hunter' would purposely blind any protester who crossed his path. Football fans were massacred in a stadium. Christians were attacked by Muslims, Muslims were set upon by Christians. No one knew who to trust. My friends developed heart palpitations, chronic coughs, headaches, agoraphobia. Where once they'd spoken to me with idealism, they now spoke with apathy. They could not watch the news.

They say that monsters exist at the edges of the world, but the world no longer has edges. Monsters exist, but they hide among us in the same cities and countries we live in, scattered across a round globe.

Sometimes, they don't even bother to hide.

Some monsters will kill you outright, or imprison you, or transform you into your basest animal self. Others will ask you awkward questions, with the surety that warriors and travelers are not often philosophers and their answers will be entertainingly incorrect. What does *al-hourayya* even mean, and how can we possibly achieve it?

I stare at the Sphinx, as others have stared at her for thousands of years, and I wonder what question she would ask me if she still spoke to travelers. I will see my habibti in just a few days, and I remember her words from the beginning of my time in Egypt.

The answer is still Man. ◼

Kaleb Blackgoat

Charlie J. Stephens

Kaleb Blackgoat came to us from his tribal land on the coast most weekends. He was a big-footed giant with enormous hands and a head chiseled out of obsidian, all angled jawline and bright eyes. When he spoke to us, his voice was deep and low, mineral-like. He was a weighted calm, settling into our little house, and he smelled of tobacco smoke and something softer: piñon or sweetgrass.

I often stood on the orange couch cushions near the front window keeping a lookout, waiting for his car to pull up: a beat-to-hell silver Ford Fairlane with a loose muffler and black, furry dice hanging from the rearview. When he walked in—it didn't matter the season, sometimes he was sweaty, sometimes we could see our breath—the first thing Kaleb did was take off his shirt, revealing his massive back. It held long-ago healed acne pockmarks and other mysterious scars, and I watched and wondered as he lay face down on the carpeted floor and called me to him. Kicking off my shoes and socks, my job was to walk all over his back; an offering, a token, a makeshift healing. My small feet slid around on his tight skin, and it was hard to stay there without falling off, toes digging in, a game to get better at, his ribs rising and falling with each breath.

Afterwards he'd pat me on the shoulder and say, Thanks kiddo, with a quiet, low laugh for what he called his rental carpet massage. Then he would leave for the kitchen where Mom was waiting. Their kissing sounded awful to me: a strange, desperate pact – a promise that would or maybe couldn't be kept.

Once I heard them talking through the thin wall between the kitchen and my bedroom, that some white men, grave robbers, had stolen some things belonging to the tribe, and that Kaleb and a friend of his were going to make it right. I drifted off, their voices lower then, dreaming of a vast green cemetery, wanting to warn them that the cedar trees would see everything, and to be careful not to get hurt.

When my mom and Kaleb broke up, without any kind of fight or door slamming, Mom told me Kaleb had left us for good, pressured by his tribe to not date white women. Mom told me everything while she threw dirty dishes into the sink, explaining how Kaleb actually had some honor and how rare that was. Defeated tears welled up as she placed her wet hands on the counter. I didn't know what to say to her, so went to sit on the orange couch, alone.

I missed him on the weekends that followed. I looked across the kitchen at the stale bread left out on the counter, looked across to the bedroom with the worn sheets in a heap, looked across the still living room at my mom, then finally down at my own pale skin. I wondered how it had taken him away from us, then wondered if his absence, instead, had something to do with the kissing. I sank into the couch, realized no one was coming, then balanced on its worn-out armrests, pretending that it was my job to stay on, no matter what. H

Ah Ya Ween (Oh, Where Am I)?

Stacy E. Holden

You pose precariously on a precipice in the High
Atlas Mountains. You don't know you will one day
find a photo of this moment tossed carelessly in a
box in the basement of your suburban home. You
don't know you will obsess for days, weeks, months
over the image just snapped by the taxi driver in
front of you.

You stand close to two women in their early-
thirties and a young hitchhiker from the Drâa
region. You have traveled for three days in a Grand
Taxi, a beat-up white Mercedes W123. Your driver is
an angular young man with a mustache who likes the
music of Nass al Ghiwane. The lyrics are still beyond
you and your recent efforts to understand Arabic,
but you are drawn to the shrill horn, the rhythmic
plucking of the banjo and the deep masculine wailing
of *Ah wa wa*. The discordant reverberations suit the
stark angles and wide spaces of the African Sahel.
Its sounds reflect the possibilities of the moment as
you start a new life in Morocco; a graduate student
researching your dissertation on urban labor in
colonial Fez. *Ah ya ween.*

In November 1999, your face is thin, your smile
broad. In a maroon t-shirt and jeans, you stand
with a casual confidence. *Ah wa wa*. You don't yet

know disordered eating and a latent but deep-seated anxiety will one day mar memories of your late-forties. You don't know you will one day gain eighty-five pounds and start to turn away from cameras, shy and ashamed. You don't know the postcard you just received from Maryclaire – picturing a naked lady in high heels bouncing across London Bridge at dawn – will one day be a story shared with high school friends attending her funeral.

The dancer, Irene, juts out her hip in lighthearted fashion. You don't know this friendship is inconsequential, despite shared meals and late-night conversations in Ouazerzate. You don't know that the boxes of photos and other mementos from that time will contain little mention of this woman. Irene holds an iguana, handed to her by a now nameless Moroccan in a badly fitting gray djellaba and black turban. *Ah wa wa.*

You stand close to Kathy, a Fulbright grantee teaching English at Hassan II University in Mohamadiyya. She complains her black wool sweater is hot and itchy and once again wishes out loud that she had worn something else that morning, just as she will nineteen years later when you text her this photo. You don't know she will return to graduate school when she goes back to the US. You don't know she will meet her husband there. You don't know they will one day visit you at a rented beach house in North Carolina and David will build sandcastles with your nervous mother. You don't know the get well card you send David on 2 July 2016 with a photo of him and that sandcastle and trite wishes for better health will reach him the day after he dies of lung cancer. *Ah ya ween.*

I should have tried to hear more than the alluring beat, to see something beyond the pretty landscape. Now fifty years old, I am in an American college town. Nondescript, at least it seems to me. I no longer climb the heights of Mount Toukbal, a massif with sedimentary rock narrating eons of historical process as worlds collided and continents formed. I look – for the fourth or four hundredth time – at that photo, now stained and curled at the sides. Seated on a deep blue loveseat, I play *Ah Ya Ween* once more, and the tinny, unfamiliar sounds surprise the cat, who wakes disoriented and angry. Soothing him, I contemplate the flexures of my own life, particularly that era when I embraced explorations of the unknown and could travel Morocco with assurance and ease. *Ah wa wa.* When did this photo become a part of my past, a primary source in my own personal archive evoking such profound nostalgia?

In the explosion of music that recalls my journey to the Drâa, I wonder if my wistful feelings are for that time or that place. Or do I just miss the naiveté, the innocence captured in the faces of the women standing so precariously on the edge of a mountain cliff? As I listen to *Ah Ya Ween*, I translate the title and recognize only now that it means 'Oh, Where Am I?' I stare at those women gathered close that November day and am drawn to their faces, to their conviction in their ability to shape the future; a belief then as measureless as the blue sky unfolding behind them. **H**

The Better Life

Bairbre Flood

Malik waited at a distribution line for shoes, a long queue reaching to the back of a van. He stood in his flip flops, and we started chatting about the winter weather; how cold it was at night in the makeshift tents. How muddy the camp was getting.

Volunteers shouted for everyone to be patient, to wait in line, but it looked like the shoes were running low and people started crushing forward – desperate to get the last of the runners – and the volunteers panicked and shut the van doors.

'I'm so sorry,' I said as the van drove away. No shoes meant no chance of jumping on the train.

'No, no, don't be upset,' Malik said. 'I didn't get shoes today, but maybe tomorrow.'

He offered me his bottle of water. 'Don't worry, maybe tomorrow.'

I took a drink and thanked him.

'There are bad people in the camp,' he whispered. 'Very bad people.'

He stayed only a few weeks longer, then applied for asylum in France and was housed at a centre for minors near Paris.

I meet him briefly, months later, in Paris for a coffee. He has a slight limp.

'I hurt it on the train,' Malik shrugs. 'But it's okay.'

He looks much older than when I'd met him in

Calais. At least then he'd had some hope. Now I don't know what he has. He stirs five sugars into his drink.

'I'm so lonely here I don't know what to do,' he says.

After surviving the Janjaweed militias, the 'demons on horses' who raped and murdered their way through his village, Malik escaped on a coffin ship from Libya; landing unwanted in Italy. He moved on to the Jungle camp in Calais, where he risked his life to climb aboard a truck, until he just couldn't take the cold and the bad people any longer, and applied for papers.

Now, finally, the end of the line. Housed in a centre in Orléans. This is it. What he'd strived for.

'No one talks to me here,' he says.

'It'll get easier. It just takes time to get used to it,' I suggest, but he shakes his head.

We talk for a while, he insists on paying for our coffee and helps me find my train. He's wearing a beautiful gold ring with a large ornate stone.

'It's from my mother,' he tells me. 'She thinks I've made it to the better life.'

On the train, I can't get his voice out of my head. I suck on throat lozenges, but I can't seem to stop my chest rattling. *No one talks to me here.* ◘

Memory City

Melissa Holbrook Pierson

The city had a weight. The force on the body,
constant but also immeasurable, was exerted by
both the abstract concept and the wholly physical
ache of yearning.

Even when I still lived there, I knew that if ever
a place embodied longing for the lost, it was New
York. Desire was the infectious agent in the air,
the vector of this disease every last window above
street level. I passed, and kept passing, as they
multiplied overhead. Tenements, lofts, high-rises.
Behind each, the life I wanted but was never going
to have. Wealth, beauty, creative genius, thrills
of such unimaginable variegation the synapses
burned. Behind the impassive glass concentrated
the memory of two hundred years of literature,
empire-making, deals and deaths, life and dinners. I
wanted in.

For a place that is constrained by geography –
boroughs that are islands, water the only ground
over which to advance new frontiers (practically
impossible, it still happens, because New York is
also a place of miracles) – the city is mystically
elastic. Hope, that which follows close upon desire, is
expansive: Maybe I will get there yet! Time balloons.
Lunch hours encompass continental explorations,
avenues and side streets charted like rivers and
mountain ranges on a map of the new world.

One walked forward into the past. Into the lunch room unchanged since 1921, with waitresses also drawn from that time.[1] Into one's own history: a small frisson—comfort as well as queasy horror— that I might be reliving my mother's life just by sitting on a stool at the counter of Chock Full o' Nuts and ordering a cream cheese on date-nut bread. (She had also moved to the same city from the same Midwestern backwater after the same college, but she returned home, defeated, after a brief career at the same employer where I would also soon get a job.) Sometimes whole decades of New York history seemed to be running simultaneously,[2] a shadow following so close on your heels it pulls your shoe off so that you look quickly back to see who is there. No one; just a doppelgänger. Let's nip in to Lord & Taylor and peruse the sales racks; after an in-depth course of study lasting the whole Fall term, they would finally

---

1 The first specimen in what I am forced to title 'A Slightly Bitter Catalog of Wistfulness' is Mary Elizabeth's, a tearoom on East 37th Street that catered to decades of ladies dining on cucumber sandwiches and Lady Baltimore cake while packing away a cocktail or two. It was located near the center of fashionable commerce, notably the great B. Altman's* department store on Fifth Avenue. Its proprietress had built an empire -- tearooms in Newport and Boston as well as New York, and sixty women toiling in a basement kitchen making sweets sold across the country -- from a candy business she started as a teen in Syracuse. She ended up with a Newport millionaire for a husband. Somehow this history, of improbability yielding to natural condition, was enclosed in the space of 6 East 37th Street. It will always be thus; you had found a place that said 'New York endures!' It closed in 1985.
 * Altman's, after existing in its imposing block-long French limestone Renaissance Revival home since 1906, closed in 1989.

2 It was less that New York City revered its history enough to preserve it; it was that no one particularly noticed that stuff was sitting around getting very, very old. You could prowl the Village in 1986, say, and see something worthy of further investigation at the end of Commerce Street and, upon entering, realize you'd stumbled on 1945. Empty of patrons, the place's waiters in long aprons and dour expressions attended to ghosts. The menu appeared on a single metal board leaning against an interior column so the staff did not have to spend any more time with you than required. Finding the place made you joyous beyond reason. The Blue Mill Tavern closed in 1992.

---

yield something in tissue silk that flew far above an editorial assistant's salary, the tag now bearing prices slashed successively from heaven to earth by the red pen of a sales clerk. See, New York was the kind of place that so fleetly elevated you to the sixteenth floor it was now you, suddenly, looking out of that window.[3]

Here is where I learned to shape-shift. High and low, sometimes in the same day. Lunch at the automated sushi joint near the office, where small white plates circulated on a conveyor belt. Hesitate, and you lost the tamago. But lo! It comes again! Could I afford three plates, or just two? There was no hiding from the voiceless waiters. You turned on your stool to catch the disdainful eye of one. In a single swift move, click click click the plates were stacked and some slashing shorthand on a check, ripped off and fluttering toward the tray where you caught it midair, then skulked to the cashier, somehow ashamed.[4]

Only in the annals of astronomy is the vastness of the New York night written, barely. This was the time of sequential transfigurations, or at least of passing. Outside a velvet rope, where a line of couples and groups stretched down the block to the vanishing point, one learned how to gather oneself up. It was, as I imagine, the feeling of a Corsair pilot in 1944, as the fighter began to

---

3 After more than a century on Fifth Avenue, Lord & Taylor shut its doors in early 2019.
4 Genroku Sushi, Fifth Avenue at 35th. $1.71 a plate. Received health code citation in 1987, closed around 1991.

shudder. He pushed the stick forward. I walked
past. Right up to the latter day Heimdall guarding
the gates of Valhalla. I barely smiled; no good to
give too much away. My stomach turned, slightly,
but nothing showed on my face. He looked to his
compatriot, who looked at me. At a short nod, the
rope was unclipped. I slipped through and it was
clipped back as quickly. As I ascended, I sensed
the perturbation in the crowd behind me. Yeah,
well. They were behind me. I was in. I tried to
memorize the feeling for future use: I belong here.
At that moment a pulsating universe took me into
its supernova. The sound came from everywhere at
once, primarily the floor. It entered by way of the
calcaneus and on up to the femur to concentrate
in the chest. The bass pounded like a heart made
external and big as Tier 3, Limelight, Pyramid.

At some point I made my way out a back door
into the cold night air again. Bent over, flipped my
long hair in front of me, and felt the winter on my
wet neck. I stayed that way a long time.

I did this outside such a deep list of clubs that
finally I was no longer able to remember if I had
ever been to Danceteria[5] or if it was my friends'
recollections that later tangled with mine. In
the city's strange ether, membranes thinned to
transparency: there was no longer any 'no' between
you and a stranger, or the year this was and another
age, or the status you woke up in this morning and

---

5 R.I.P. 1986. The great Mudd Club had closed three years earlier, but CBGB hung
on until 2006. Its storied squalor was replaced by a high-end men's clothier.

the one you would assume by dinnertime. One foot in your own life, the next step already reaching toward another's. Whose? Yours? The person you were becoming? The person who passed you on the subway stairs?

Even my dreams reversed places with whatever I was used to calling reality. The pressure of those shorelines, rivers to either side, harbor below, pushed relentlessly on the notion of space. The crown prince of New York was real estate. Everyone thought about it, continuously. I coveted every place I entered, re-casting myself from the girl who lived in a mouse-and-roach-infested three-room floor-through with dropped ceilings so low my taller guests had to take an immediate seat (and there were only three). There was dinner with the editor of a famous literary monthly in her Upper West Side apartment. It had a rolling library ladder to attain the tops of bookshelves that lined a double-height living room. In the hall off the dining room I found the oak panel that was actually a door to that mythical space known as a powder room – just for guests – so I could sob unseen over an imagined slight, or perhaps the knowledge that I would never have two-story bookshelves. There were visits with the parents of my college roommate in the Park Avenue apartment so large I got lost in it; the maid's room was off the kitchen but of course their maid only came in during the day so it was empty. They took me to the Rainbow Room for Easter. It now hosts New Year's Eve parties at $1,650 per person. Someone – a friend of a friend of a friend (the access routes to lofty precincts as likely to disappear as soon as they had appeared) – lived in the octagonal cupola atop a building in Tribeca, windows all around and the breeze slowly animating a tropical rainforest in pots on the rooftop patio outside. That was real estate, all right: the entire sky. I knew someone who lived in the black-and-white tiled bathroom of what had once been a grand place — or did I dream that?

It was in the middle of the night that all remaining seams came fully undone. I dreamed of the places in which I really lived, none of them the succession of scabby, unrenovated tenements that I actually inhabited. Even if these had smelled of lemon polish and one could hear the Miele vacuum faintly in the distance as the maid did her daily diligence on the hand-knotted silk orientals, I would have dreamed of spaces with still higher ceilings. How was it I did not know there was a thousand-square-foot walnut-paneled library, furnished in leather club chairs and Tiffany table lamps, two-story-tall windows hung with olive-green velvet drapes, behind the closet shoved under the staircase in my $450-a-month slum? How did I miss the fact that there was a Moroccan-tiled Olympic-size swimming pool in the basement that I was unaware sat below the fossilized kitchen linoleum? I can see these vast echoing spaces more vividly now than I can recall the four apartments in which I had truly lived, not forgetting the sorry rentals of three boyfriends.

Once I dreamed of visiting an office – my point

of view on entrance apparently that of Orson Welles in 1941, with a fifty-foot depth of field to the fireplace and oak desk at the other end – and when I woke felt strange. I wanted nothing so much as to return, yet it was more unreachable a destination than Jupiter's moons: It was locked in me.

A few years later, flipping through a magazine, suddenly there it was. Impossible. The place I had visited in a dream. But if it was in New York Magazine, nothing could be more real. In Grand Central, the epic cathedral of an office had been closed away for four decades, since the death of its occupant, John Campbell. Now it was being turned into a bar (after the application of $1.5 million in developer's lucre, a mere portion of the worth of the massive Persian rug that had once covered its floor and had disappeared[6]). Campbell had died the year I was born.

Not only did New York elide years and lives, possibilities and memories; it ripped the last veil separating the real from the immaterial. I moved there the fall after college. Actually, I didn't; I could only afford somewhere called Hoboken. This was not, I belatedly learned, a neighborhood in Manhattan.

Hoboken was separated from the only place that mattered by a river, the Hudson. One simply had to lean at a 45-degree angle into the freezing wind

---

6 The rush to remake even that which has been recently remade -- after something old has been rediscovered in today's New York, it cannot be ripped up fast enough to be replicated into a cleaner, smoother simulacrum of its original handmade self -- is illustrated here by the Campbell Apartment bar. The 1999 renovation lasted only eight years before it was in need of freshening; an additional $350,000 was spent on new fittings that were installed in 12 hours, so not a single night of revelry was lost. It has since closed again.

tunnel of the streets – by my third apartment there, almost a mile of them, still farther into the deep ruins of this forgotten old town – and think hard of the PATH station. Down the stairs the pillowy embrace of warm air awaited. All you had to do was slip a dollar bill into the turnstile. One train headed to the World Trade Center, the other to Christopher, 9th, 14th, 23rd, 33rd Streets. Given the laggardly schedule, if you heard a train coming while still cursing at a limp bill, there was no choice. You jumped over the gate and flew down the stairs to the platform. Your punishment was frequently to throw yourself onto the departing train only to find, after the doors closed, that it was heading to Newark.

Our small tribe of Hoboken non-natives huddled together for warmth at the few going concerns in our adopted town, Maxwell's preeminent among them. The nature of Hoboken as hovering psychically somewhere near that line, spelled out in tile in the middle of the Holland Tunnel, between New York and New Jersey was captured in The New Yorker's squib on the small but influential music club: BEST CLUB IN NEW YORK — EVEN THOUGH IT'S IN NEW JERSEY. You didn't necessarily know anything about the band you were going to hear on Friday night, but you went because it was Maxwell's and because it was always interesting, if occasionally atonal. Plus it was the only place open in a town that pulled down metal shutters en masse no later than 6 pm. After the event you might discover you'd witnessed a segment of rock history that would be canonized in a music writer's book about the 'scene'. It turned out you were living in important times, in an important place.[7]

The act of rushing down the long passageway at the 9th Street station, the one in which I found myself at the end of uncountable nights of after-parties and clubs, has made the odor of roasting lamb with rosemary and garlic – courtesy of the exhaust vents from the Balducci's above the station[8] – a touchstone for a thousand memories.

A thousand more remain buried where I can't quite get at them. I don't know what cabinet in me is big enough to store them, but where else could they have gone? They might be found bound to my molecules, like those pieces of exploded stars, thirteen billion years old, in the mineral atoms of my blood. It is no less impossible to think of myself as composed of the residue of ten and a half million minutes lived in New York City as of the Big Bang: all life traced

---

7 After a dry run at closure in 2013 followed by another attempt, Maxwell's ceased to exist in 2018, after thirty years.

8 There used to be only one Balducci's, as it once used to be in New York. When I moved there I somehow assumed there was a law prohibiting national chains from operating within the city, or maybe simply the collective good sense of the populace to eschew them. When McDonald's began, incredibly, to proliferate in the city, it turns out my naïve assumption was more or less correct: in 1995 Mayor Giuliani, the man responsible for 'cleaning up' New York, redrew zoning plans and caused whole neighborhoods to become suburban strip malls.
A small Italian grocer's opened in Manhattan in 1916, and occupying the Sixth Avenue store since the 1970s, Balducci's was the Tiffany's of foodstuffs. It offered the impoverished ingénue the opportunity to wander its aisles and imagine the day when she would be able to toss French cheeses and cipollini onions into her basket without a thought as to cost. Then, in a trajectory so predictable it would be sad if it were not such a cliché, Balducci's in the nineties started experiencing a Napoleonic urge toward empire. It was sold to a Maryland-based, company, and the 9th Street store was closed in 2003. It drew back the curtain on its new and improved future by reopening (naturally) in a grand old bank building on 14th Street. It had readied itself for purchase by an actual bank. Of course, the store was soon deemed 'underperforming.' It closed two years later. Now Balducci's exists everywhere (if one considers Greenwich, Scarsdale, and JFK everywhere), but not Manhattan.

back to these. Now the memories comprise the only me it is possible to be after so many years in New York, every minute of which is worth a whole day somewhere else. I brushed unknowingly against greatness – the famous and brilliant whose sweat was flung onto my own skin in the loud dimness of the Mudd Club, CBGB, Madame Rosa's – and the not so great, finding much later I had probably jammed my elbow into the back of the man I was years later to marry and then divorce . How much happened in the dark, at night.

We rushed to, and into, it all. Life's directory was The Village Voice,[9] its listings commensurately thick with possibility, inked and over-inked every week in hope. We did not precisely understand what hope it was, only that we were awash in it. It was so big that it could not have a name, just as the place we lived in refused all demarcations. But an engine was running perpetually in the background, its sound barely noticeable for its constancy.

We were all looking for someone. Through all the gallery openings, film lectures, clubs, gang dinners, writing alone in cafes, parties after which you'd stand on the platform at 3 am exhausted out of your mind, wishing it was all over, or at least that you hadn't missed a train five minutes before. Looking for someone was not the reason we went out – the magnificence of New York was the reason we went out, the peripheral consciousness that we were living at some high point of cultural history, and were

---

9 Publication ceased 2018.

therefore participating in its manufacture – but it was the hum that ran night and day underneath our feet, like the subway below the apparently solid ground on which we walked. We were looking for someone so we could stop going out. We would not leave New York, for that was not possible. New York would leave us.

After eleven years in Hoboken, I moved to Brooklyn. The next ten years, I see only now, comprised a long process of untethering myself from longing, from New York.

The original people of New York were the Lenape Indians. It is not necessary to offer details, because their story is the repeated story of every aboriginal people in the land we call ours: war, treaty, broken treaty, sale of place that could not really be such when they had no concept for ownership of their heaven, the earth. Nonetheless, it was bought for sixty guilders. Then they had to leave.

Like all who go, they left something behind. Broadway, the pathway worn by millennia of soft-shod footsteps, was overlaid by the histories of those who came later, and those who came later yet. But because it is New York, the sound of the Indians' going can still be heard, simultaneous with the clangor of sequential millions along their route. Somewhere, perhaps even now in someone's dream, it is 1983 and a young woman is climbing the steps from the subway, looking up to find the Twin Towers to orient herself toward downtown. She is going to a party she heard about via electrical impulses passed among friends. Past darkfall, she walks alone down empty Lispenard Street, watching for a single row of lights on a fourth floor. The only thing she knows is that there she will meet some form of fate. Her exhaled breath, I think, still forms part of the atmosphere over the city to which people come, and people go. ◲

여유

Yeoyu ——
new voices
Korea

Han Kang
Bae Suah
Han Yujoo
Kim Soom
Kang Hwagil
Jeon Sungtae
Cheon Heerahn
Hwang Jungeun

CHEON HEERAHN

다섯 개의 프
렐류드, 그리
고 푸가

천희란
이예원

FIVE
PRELUDES
& A FUGUE

TRANSLATED BY EMILY YAE WON

EUROPA

한강

에우
로파

데브라
스미스

HAN KANG

TRANSLATED BY DEBORAH SMITH

DIVOR
CE KIM
SOOM

이혼 김숨

TRANSLATED BY EMILY YAE WON

전성태
JEON SUNGTAE

퇴역 레슬러

OLD WRESTLER

BAE SUAH
배수아

MILENA,
MILENA,
ECSTATIC

TRANSLATED BY DEBORAH SMITH

한유주 HAN YUJOO

LEFT'S
RIGHT

왼쪽의
오른쪽

RIGHT'S
LEFT

자넷 홍

오른쪽
의왼쪽

TRANSLATED BY JANET HONG

Pileated In Humboldt County

by John Van Kirk

Eyes wide and shiny, smiling beatifically to himself, Ray was sitting cross-legged on the floor of his dorm room listening to The Moody Blues. He had all their albums stacked on his turntable, and although he was playing them in the order of their release, I was shocked that he could listen to all the A-sides and then all the B-sides, instead of listening to each album the way it was meant to be played, as I saw it. But considering that he was tripping on acid, I thought I'd let it go. This was our first meeting, taking place during the first week of our freshman year at Webster College in St. Louis, a thousand miles away from New Jersey, where we both had grown up.

I had come to Webster alone, knowing no one. Ray had come with his friend since third grade, Bill, who had already become my first college friend. It was in the natural order of things that Ray and I should also become friends. In time I would become close to many of Bill and Ray's circle in New Jersey, meeting some of them that first Christmas, when we went back east to spend the holidays with our folks. There were lots of basement parties that season with beer, wine, weed, and the occasional hallucinogen. It was the winter of 1970. The girls wore their hair long and straight; the boys carried draft cards in their wallets.

We were all skinny in those days, but Ray had a loose-jointed way of moving and the wide hips that already suggested the big man he would become. With features carved of beechwood and red cedar, hair the color of straw, Ray was a ginger long before that word came back into fashion. He favored faded jeans and flannel shirts, and in all the years I knew him I don't think I ever saw him lose his temper. Bill and I rode back to St. Louis that winter in Ray's yellow VW bus, which broke down on the way. Bill and I were not much help, but Ray kept his cool, somehow got a perfect stranger to help him fix the van, and got us back to Webster before spring classes started up.

It was the winter of 1970. The girls wore their hair long and straight; the boys carried draft cards in their wallets

By the time we were sophomores, it was clear that college was not for Ray. A practical man, who understood tools and was good with his hands, a reader who would happily converse about books and ideas, he was not one to write analytical term papers or allow himself to be measured by his knowledge of what he considered trivial: names and dates and facts he didn't think he'd ever really need to know. At some point Ray drove the VW back to New Jersey and found a job as an apprentice woodworker in a furniture shop, where he learned the carpentry and furniture-making skills that he would continue to use for the rest of his life. Some years later he moved out to Garberville, California, where Ray collected his mail from a post office box and had no phone, off the grid before there was a grid. He built timber homes, made fine furniture, and grew cannabis; small clusters of plants hidden deep within copses of poison oak, carefully pruned and nurtured, irrigated by an intricate system of his own design.

Ray ... had no phone, off the grid before there was a grid. He built timber homes, made fine furniture and grew cannabis

Long after college, that East Coast circle of friends would still get together around Christmas time. We met up in New Jersey, each of us returning from our far-flung adult lives like the Swallows to Capistrano. 'Is Ray coming this year,' someone would always ask, because, in addition to wanting to see our old friend, everybody knew that Ray – flying in from Humboldt County – would arrive bearing a suitcase full of the best weed money could buy. I had joined the Navy by then, and could not partake, but the quality of Ray's product was evident in its sticky buds, its piney aroma, the smell of its smoke, and the hilarity that followed its passage around a room.

Ray's place in the redwoods had acquired a mythical status. Those who had visited spoke highly of the piece of land he owned, the house he had built and furnished with his own hands, and the high-grade crop he tended. I visited him there twice, the first time when the Navy had stationed me in Monterey for a few months, and though I couldn't smoke with him, I enjoyed his company, his cooking, and the quiet seclusion of his home. He took me out to his workshop, where I watched sawdust fly as he worked on a coffee table he had been commissioned to make. I made use of his recently completed composting toilet that was set strategically into the hillside – to give its occupant a panoramic view of the misty mountains. And he showed me his plans for a sauna.

When I found myself in California again a few years later, now an aspiring writer, no longer in the Navy, I made sure I found time to go see Ray again.

Among the pursuits I had taken up after leaving the service was birdwatching, and when I headed up to Humboldt County, I had just taken possession of my first pair of quality binoculars. Ravens, which I could now distinguish from Crows, passed overhead as I drove the washboard road out to Ray's home high in the mountain woods. The next day, Ray took me out to the coast, where I added the Osprey and the Black Oystercatcher to the life-list I had recently begun. Back at his place, I heard the plaintive and haunting song of the Hermit Thrush in the trees, though I never got a good look at one; and Ray kept telling me of the Pileated Woodpeckers he routinely saw in the clearing behind his house.

'They feed on the ants in the rotting logs and dead trees,' he said, pointing out a standing dead tree that the birds had carved into almost sculptural shapes. I wanted desperately to see this bird, dramatically described in my field guide as 'a spectacular, *crow-sized* woodpecker with a flaming red *crest*.' Occasionally we would hear the cry of what I thought must be some kind of hawk, and Ray would say, 'There's the Pileated.' The drumming that followed confirmed Ray's identification. But I never caught a glimpse of it.

The day before I was to leave was crisp and clear; it was June, and we were up above 3000 feet. Ray invited me to join him in the sauna, which he had completed since my last visit, arranging the stones for its foundation and fireplace, sawing and setting the logs that made up its walls, and planing local madrone for the floor, the benches, and the door. He was proud of his work, as he was proud of his pot. He lit a fire that heated up an iron tray of stones, and while we waited for the sauna to warm up, he held out a joint. I had not smoked weed in nearly ten years. But there were no drug tests in my future, and the joint that he flourished before me smelled wonderful. I took a toke, coughed like a rank amateur as Ray looked on, and then I took another, more carefully this time, and held it. As I let the smoke out, I already felt the high move through me like a gust of wind. We stripped down, piled our clothes on the picnic table, and ducked into the sauna.

I am not the biggest fan of saunas. I don't mind sweating from exercise, or even moderate heat, but

I don't like to feel as if I am being cooked. Seeming to sense my discomfort, Ray ladled cold water from a bucket onto the hot stones. The sauna filled with a cloud of steam, and I wasn't at all sure this was an improvement.

At about the time I thought I couldn't stand another minute, Ray said, 'Let's take a break.' As we stepped outside, steam rose from our bodies, and we heard that hawk-like call.

Black and shiny as a crow, its crest red as fire, the white markings on its face and neck standing out as bright as fresh paint

'It's the Pileated,' Ray said. 'Over there.' And he pointed to a black and red shape hammering on the trunk of a fallen pine.

My binoculars were on the table with our clothes, and I picked them up and peered through them, focusing in on the biggest woodpecker I had ever seen, black and shiny as a crow, its crest red as fire, the white markings on its face and neck standing out as bright as fresh paint, the scene made even more impressive with the 8.5 magnification. Wood chips flew as the bird – a carpenter like Ray, I thought – drilled industriously into the ochre-colored wood. Then, high for the first time in so many years, I seemed to move briefly outside myself, taking it all in, the deep warmth of my own body, fresh from the sauna, the invigorating chill of the mountain air, and the sight, as if I were watching from above, of two steaming naked men standing in a clearing in the woods, gaping at an almost comically outsized woodpecker as it energetically tore a downed tree trunk to pieces.

Later I entered the Pileated Woodpecker onto my life list. Ray and I enjoyed the long evening together, watching the sun go down through the floor-to-ceiling windows of his living room, dining well at the table he had made, and sharing a bottle of good red wine. The next day I headed back to my artist's residency in the Santa Cruz mountains, well south of the range of the Pileated Woodpecker, where I was trying to write a book of stories set in New Jersey, three thousand miles away.

We lost Ray not too many years after that. Cancer. I remember him as one of the rare ones who chose the life he wanted and lived the life he chose, rather than a life that had been chosen for him. His name has now been added to the list we least like making. But his name also appears on my life-list:

> Pileated Woodpecker, male, feeding on carpenter ants. June 1992, late afternoon. With Ray at his place, Humboldt County, CA.

Here he is still very much alive, sharing a piece of his world with me as we stand side-by-side in the forest our naked bodies steaming, shimmering with delight at the sight of a marvelous bird. ◪

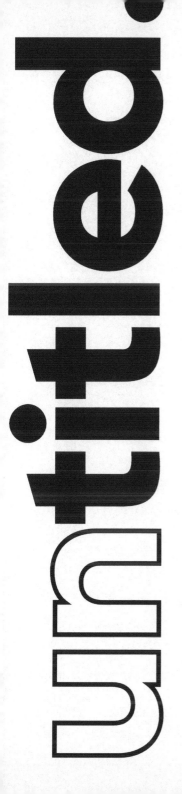

You thought you knew the whole story...

Come and celebrate with us at Untitled writers' events - a new platform for underrepresented writers to share their work in front of an audience. There are no limitations to what might be shared and we know there'll be something for everyone.

To find out more about Untitled, let us know if you want to share your work in the future and to find news about our next event visit **untitledwriting.co.uk**

 writinguntitled   untitled_writing

Who Will Believe Thee?

What Shakespeare Shows Us about Sexual Misconduct in the Current Climate

by Cynthia Lewis

As the action thickens in Shakespeare's *Measure for Measure*, Isabella – about to declare herself a novice nun – leaves the convent on a summons to beg for the life of her imprisoned brother Claudio. He has impregnated his wife-to-be, which barely qualifies as a crime in either Shakespeare's England or seventeenth-century Vienna, the play's setting. But Angelo, a humorless, frigid deputy left in charge of governing while the rightful Duke has left the city, takes it upon himself to punish all the sexuality he considers the least bit errant, and Claudio's premarital intercourse is prominently displayed on Juliet's protruding womb. When Angelo sentences Claudio to death for his behavior, Isabella approaches him in his chamber, marshaling as much theology as she can to dissuade him from judging a man for sexual urges that, she submits, Angelo must feel himself. But in fact, not until a woman of such chaste virtue as Isabella pleads with him does the repressed Angelo begin to awaken sexually. After their first meeting, Angelo sends Isabella away, then confesses to the audience that he's in her thrall. When she returns the next day, at his bidding, he bribes her: he'll let her brother live if she 'gives him love.'

Incredulous at Angelo's hypocrisy, Isabella threatens him with public exposure. 'Sign me a present pardon for my brother,' she demands, 'Or with outstretch'd throat I'll tell the world aloud / What man thou art.' Angelo's response seems as fresh at this present moment as it must have in 1603. 'Who will believe thee, Isabel?' He proceeds to bully her with his perfect reputation.

> My unsoil'd name, th' austereness of my life,
> My vouch against you, and my place i' th' state,
> Will so your accusation overweigh,
> That you shall stifle in your own report,
> And smell of calumny.

After further intimidating her, he exits, leaving Isabella to parrot his question. 'To whom should I complain?' she asks herself. 'Did I tell this, / Who would believe me?'

Isabella's world being a play – and a quirky kind of comedy at that – she is eventually believed. For the Duke is only pretending to be absent from Vienna and has remained, disguised, to spy on Angelo, who quickly discloses himself to the Duke's covert observation. At a public gathering in the play's last scene, the Duke arranges a prolonged exposure of Angelo's sexual misconduct, so humiliating Angelo that he begs to be executed and freeing Isabella from the ill repute Angelo once held over her. The story of how Isabella's quid pro quo sexual harassment dilemma is resolved is a fantasy many women share in the here and now: irrefutable evidence. No male complicity machine. A publicly shamed harasser and a champion who sees justice delivered.

But before the Duke allows the truth about Angelo's sexual aggression toward Isabella to come out, he pretends in front of the crowd that he doesn't believe her. He questions her sanity for so much as accusing the presumably upright Angelo, and he allows Angelo to question her 'wits.' By the time the Duke reveals that he knows she's truthful and reviles Angelo's conduct, she has been dragged through pitch. The man who releases Isabella from Angelo's lies first exercises an obscene amount of control over her. Then, just as the play is closing, the Duke proposes marriage to Isabella, who, as shocked as the audience is, doesn't respond. In the end, she's silenced again.

———

Reflecting on this play, I'm trying to piece together my own history of sexual harassment and assault.

My first commencement ceremony at the college where, 38 years later, I still teach was coming to a close. As everyone rose from their seats to go their separate ways, I was tackled to the ground by one of the graduates. Stunned and pinned down by his body, I couldn't escape. Two male faculty colleagues pulled him off of me, helped me up, and apologized that my first commencement as a new faculty member should have been so marred. That was it. Possibly, the college's President added his apology to that of the others; I can't recall all the details. What I'm certain of is that the man who assaulted me went on to law school, practices law to this day in Tennessee, and enjoys recurring gigs as a play-by-play radio basketball announcer. Back in May of 1981, he had been stalking several women – most of them college employees like me – during the days before commencement, exhibiting behavior that ought to have been examined closely by senior college officials, who were aware of it.

> **What I'm certain of is that the man who assaulted me went on to law school, practices law to this day in Tennessee, and enjoys recurring gigs as a play-by-play radio basketball announcer**

The only excuse I can imagine for those administrators – all of whom were men – is that they thought we women were adults who could take care of ourselves. But that outlook, as reasonable and refreshingly non-patronizing as it may seem, doesn't address how this man, who was obviously ill, got waived into the legal system. While researching his current whereabouts and occupation, I came across an article in his local newspaper regarding three misdemeanor charges he was served in 2005. He was accused of aggravated criminal trespassing, simple assault, and vandalism when, incensed that his mother hadn't been mailed her automobile registration renewal form in two years, he erupted in rage at the county courthouse and shoved the county mayor. Said his lawyer, 'From my investigation of the relevant surrounding facts, it appears that this unfortunate incident is being blown out of proportion.'

I knew I would hear almost identical words from my male colleagues if, back in 1981, I had complained about being thrown to the ground by that graduating senior. Rather than cause a fuss, I kept my peace.

—

In 2004, I was teaching one of my favorite classes, 'Shakespeare and His Contemporaries,' in which perhaps twenty brave souls had enrolled to study the likes of Christopher Marlowe, Thomas Heywood, and Thomas Middleton, alongside the only name they likely recognized. Well into the Fall semester, I started receiving lewd emails from the name 'noya clap,' who was clearly a member of the drama class. I don't use the word lewd frivolously. Here's a sample:

> look cynthia i am trying to be nice to you
> and you are being such an arrogant bitch.
> i saw you wearing those high boots today,
> you should have worn a mini skirt so i could
> see your panties. . . . one time i went to the
> bathroom and whacked off thinking about
> your sweaty pussy on my balls, so at least
> wear some low cut skirt and a tank top with
> no bra ok, thanks darling

Although I knew which student 'noya clap' was, I had no proof; nailing down enough evidence to have him removed from my class and initiate proceedings against him involved the Dean of Students, the college's President, the chief of campus police, and a college-retained lawyer, who was the only woman on my support team. After several sleepless nights and several days in class spent trying to keep my cool as my teaching tanked, the head of campus police, working with a retired FBI computer analyst, traced the emails to a service provider. Now the lawyer could procure a warrant for the account information that would identify 'noya clap.'

Before this point, the President, intending to rescue me, had repeatedly offered to appear in my class and demand that 'noya clap' come forward. That approach, I worried aloud, would disrupt one of the most delightful, finely tuned discussion classes I'd ever had the pleasure to teach. I was determined not to let the other students know what was going on. I politely declined the President's offer. Eventually the student was identified and, as he awaited his father's arrival to take him home, was under a restraining order not to set foot on campus. That's when he wrote me a long letter that he gave to the President to deliver to me. Despite the restraining order, the President (with good intentions, I'm sure) delivered the letter, in which the student wrote that, if he could only look into my eyes, he could convince me how sorry he was to have upset me. He was continuing to stalk me through the person who had most power to stop him, but who couldn't see how he was prolonging my distress.

—

The summer after I'd graduated from college, I went to my undergraduate mentor's house for a tutorial on a reading list for my first year in graduate school that included several difficult works in his field. I had been to his home many times, both for social gatherings and to babysit his two children. By this point, I was friends with his wife. On that warm afternoon, he and I met in his basement study and discussed obscure poems by Edmund Spenser. As I got up to leave and headed for the door, he grabbed me and forced himself on me. I was paralyzed. I could hear his wife's footfall overhead. For fear of upsetting her, I couldn't make myself call out.

But that wasn't all that stopped me from vigorously fighting him off. I was staggered. How could he be doing this to me? For three years, I had trusted him without reserve. I had opened my mind to him, bombed at intellectual risks I'd taken with him, and gratefully benefited from his recommendations to graduate schools. During those three years of believing he had my best interests at heart, he'd been grooming me, waiting for the opportunity to take advantage of my vulnerability. He knew I felt beholden to him. In a moment, my trust vanished, leaving the stench of betrayal. Over forty years later, I'm trying to clear the air, but still wondering, 'to whom should I complain?'

—

Although I've never faced stakes as dire as Shakespeare's Isabella, whose brother's life is on the line, the three adverse sexual encounters I've sketched are dire enough. They aren't the sum total of my own experiences, nor are they uncommon. Most people I know can recount at least as many that are at least as grim.

These stories inevitably include the salient elements of *Measure for Measure*. A man given virtually limitless power wastes no time leveraging it over a vulnerable, young female with virtually no power and a need he can fulfill. Her rescue from that official is managed entirely by another man, also a public authority, who exacts his own price. As part of his plot to expose her abuser, the Duke persuades Isabella to pretend publicly that she has in fact slept with Angelo, and he tells her, falsely, that her brother has been executed, the better to manipulate her emotions. In addition, his clandestine means of gathering information about her and of coming to her aid (at one point, another character refers to him as the 'Duke of dark corners') savor of the very perversion that saturates Angelo's underhandedness. Although from one perspective the Duke is Angelo's antithesis and Isabella's true redeemer, from another angle he appears a stalker, who achieves physical and even spiritual closeness to Isabella by masquerading as a celibate friar.

Perhaps the most striking parallel between the world of Shakespeare's play and our own is how densely and inescapably male is a woman's path to justice. In *Measure for Measure*, the only way to avoid being violated – to dodge the predations of an Angelo – is, at best, to rely upon male authority and, at worst, to be further compromised by it. That configuration also characterizes a majority of recent cases, in which nearly all of the responses to female complainants who have garnered attention in the media have been made by powerful men.

What may seem like a new era is but an inching forward in a nation that three years ago elected a President who boasts of grabbing women's bodies

The myriad ways that a 400-year-old play eerily reflects our culture back to us should tell us something. Although terms like 'turning point,' 'watershed,' and 'breakthrough' have been repeatedly invoked to describe the remarkable revelations about sexual abuses in recent months – and although they are truly remarkable relative to recent years – what may seem like a new era is but an inching forward in a nation that three years ago elected a President who boasts of grabbing women's bodies. Neither dismissing the movement toward justice as inconsequential nor failing to harness its energy toward ever more profound and pervasive change is productive. But neglecting its limitations carries its own hazards. As in the cases of Bill Cosby, Harvey Weinstein and others, not until legions of women asserted themselves was any one of them able to make a dent in the patriarchal bloc sustained in part by unconscious oblivion and partly by willful denial. Many of those women (and some men), moreover, have been celebrities or have joined together to expose a celebrity. As the Supreme Court hearings involving Christine Blasey Ford's accusations toward Brett Kavanaugh indicated, millions of less visible people still await their own reckoning.

What's more, as those hearings also attest, belief in complaints remains problematic. The relatively low incidence of false reporting about a sexual assault – according to FBI statistics, from two to eight per cent – is not well known. Just one false report alone, as in the instance of the *Rolling Stone* debacle, when a reporter failed to verify an accuser's story, taints the credibility of the majority of valid complaints. Even the suggestion of false reporting, which hovered over Blasey Ford, can coat all such complaints with suspicion. But statistics gathered by the FBI and organizations like RAINN (Rape, Abuse & Incest National Network) suggest that the more pronounced challenge of reporting sexual assault is not false claims, but, rather, under-reporting. Eighteen percent of women in the U.S. are raped in their lifetimes; only about a third of those report their rapes.

When Blasey Ford came forward with her report of sexual assault, in another arena dominated by men, Brett Kavanaugh, presuming the privilege of calling the confirmation process a 'national disgrace,' met her with fierce accusations of falsehood and conspiracy on the order of Angelo's response to Isabella. He barked down his opponents. Some supporters, whose initial feints suggested their belief in Blasey Ford's story, ultimately turned to the elegant but specious conclusion that Dr. Ford had been traumatized, but, apparently, by someone else.

I've been using the terms rape and assault advisedly to point out another kink in the road toward a victim's being believed. Critics of reactions to recent revelations of sexual abuse cite the wide spectrum of what qualifies as sexual misconduct to caution against rallying around each and every complaint. Cultural critic Judith Levine, known for her controversial 2002 book *Harmful to Minors: The Perils of Protecting Children from Sex*, warns in an article in *The Boston Review*, 'We are . . . flattening distinctions.' She notes the wide disparity between what Garrison Keillor describes as an 'unintentional touch' on a woman's 'bare back' and Harvey Weinstein's gallery of horrors against innumerable women. Keillor, who for over forty years hosted *A Prairie Home Companion on Minnesota Public Radio*, was dismissed, laments Levine, not for an instance of genuine sexual abuse, but because of an accident for which he apologized to the woman in question. Treating credulity toward women's stories of abuse as a wrong-headed social movement, Levine writes, 'To Believe Women … is to disbelieve, and deny due process to, the accused.' Aligning with Masha Gessen, who wrote 'When Does a Watershed Become a Sex Panic?' for *The New Yorker* in 2017, Levine peppers her admonitions about treating all sexual harassers and offenders alike with such vocabulary as 'mania,' 'panic,' 'hysteria,' and, in a sarcastic reference to the lashing of men who have committed but a modest indiscretion, 'Jacobin purge.'

Surely Levine and others of her persuasion have a point – a couple, in fact. First, lumping together all sexual offenses is simply unfair and, at worst, unproductive. As Levine argues, it can lead to women losing political and social ground, not least because it makes women seem undiscerning and overly sensitive. To take such offense at Al Franken's alleged groping of Leeann Tweeden as to demand his resignation from the Senate is potentially to collapse an instance of bad judgment with more extreme forms of sexual violence like rape into one indistinct pile. Jane Mayer's recent micro-analysis of this case in *The New Yorker*, which includes many voices who feel the evidence against Franken was inconclusive and believe he was robbed of due process, speaks to this concern. Second, believing a woman's charge of sexual misconduct without benefit of thorough and unbiased investigation stands to victimize the accused.

Levine peppers her admonitions about treating all sexual harassers and offenders alike with such vocabulary as 'mania,' 'panic,' 'hysteria'

This possibility has long been a perceived flaw on college campuses, which have been held strictly to structures built into Title IX law. One of Betsy DeVos's first concerns as the newly appointed Secretary of Education under Donald Trump was to address the rights of those accused of sexual misconduct on college and university campuses, most of them college men, in Title IX investigations. Automatically believing women's complaints, worry DeVos, Levine, and others, is tantamount to a scare. Rather than innocent until proven guilty, the accused are presumed guilty and are robbed of the ability to defend themselves and of access to unbiased judgment. The recent complaint lodged publicly against comedian Aziz Ansari reflects both the confusion over what, exactly, constitutes sexual assault and the importance of hearing the accused person's side of the story.

What extending such rights to the accused on college campuses can mean, however, is robbing complainants of their rights, subjecting them to ongoing trauma. College women who report sexual misconduct often find themselves in classes with the men in question and will likely run into those men at some point, particularly on a small campus, perhaps at a social gathering. Many of those encounters may prove benign, but others intimidate and upset students who still feel violated and threatened. Of course, some accused people are mistreated, but the antidote to their mistreatment is not the wholesale distrust of complainants and their reports or, for that matter, reducing offenses to lapses of judgment or behavior that, after all, isn't really that bad.

What's more, preferential treatment of some men who are the subjects of complaints is well known to arise, especially for some children of alumni, donors' children and, notably, athletes. Brock Turner's case from 2015 displayed several particulars of the thickly wooded area that often insulates men from accountability for their sexual misconduct. Turner, a swimmer at Stanford

University, himself drunk at the time, sexually assaulted a woman who had passed out near a dumpster. ('Sexual assault' doesn't faithfully reflect Turner's penetrating her digitally.) In a letter to the court, he excused himself for bad judgment as a result of drinking too much, which he said he thought a real college student was supposed to do. His father's letter to the court objected to his son's three guilty verdicts by reference to only '20 minutes of action out of his twenty plus years of life.' Judge Aaron Persky, a former Stanford athlete himself, worried that a steep sentence would have a 'severe impact' on Turner, so he ignored prosecutors' recommendation of six years in prison and gave him up to six months, which he could shave down to three months with good behavior. (In June 2018, Judge Persky was recalled from office, the first time since 1932 that a sitting judge in California has been recalled.)

Where complaints of sexual harassment and assault are concerned, by far the most common scenario is that even a single complaint turns out to be not only valid, but linked to other, similarly disturbing incidents. Garrison Keillor, whose dismissal prompted so much wailing and gnashing of teeth, was investigated by Minnesota Public Radio and was found, in fact, to have a history of sexual predation both on the job and off. He posted this limerick about an undergraduate employee in his bookstore, which had recently moved onto the Macalester College campus:

A beauty who goes to Macalester —
O, her face, her limbs, her ballast, her
Tiny blue kilt
And the way she is built
Could make a petrified phallus stir.

Here are all the essentials: a powerful employer
with the option of firing an employee who doesn't
appreciate sexual attention from a man about four
times her age. Macalester became aware of the
situation and did nothing about it; to take action
would jeopardize the college's relationship with
a revered Minnesotan, however tarnished his
celebrity. Imagine being the subject of those kinky
lines. Would anyone in that employee's position
ever feel safe working in that bookstore again? The
limerick may not be on the order of a rape, but it's
about as creepy a violation of her personhood as
could be conceived – rather like the image of Al
Franken cupping his hands around the sleeping
Leeann Tweeden's breasts.

Keillor's and Franken's examples are not micro-
aggressions, nor are reactions to them the stuff of
hysteria. They are instances of full-fledged sexual
misconduct. Both Franken and Keillor have origins
in writing and delivering edgy, mocking comedy
– comedy that can seem to de-fang its message
while actually enhancing its bite. Both men couch
their crude treatment of the women in question in
humor – often ostensibly self-deprecating humor
– at the expense of their targets. If they can make
their audiences laugh at an erection or by helping

themselves to handfuls of a woman's flesh, then where's the harm? But make no mistake. They are causing harm. My college mentor, who assaulted me on my way out of his house, didn't penetrate me vaginally, but rubbing himself on my thigh as he pinned me against the wall and pretending (I think) to have an orgasm was plenty upsetting. To view my resulting distress as a kind of 'mania' is itself maniacal.

In response to labeling of the #MeToo movement as a 'sex panic,' Anne McClintock, professor of gender and sexuality studies at Princeton, writes: 'There is a sex panic – a sex panic of privileged men who feel their power slipping. (And we must repeat #NotAllMen.) Panic ignites into violence at the flashpoints of wounded masculinity: in trolls threatening to rape, mutilate, and murder women, in the Gamergate haters, and in revenge porn.'

A staple response to the threat of losing power is pretending that the abuse of power is benign. Another staple is denying that abuse ever occurred and treating the accuser as a liar or a hysteric or, at the very least, an unreliable, and therefore easily subverted, source.

———

Stories of sexual misconduct are overflowing the levy, seeping out of every crevice, and flooding the media, are overwhelming in their volume. How did we get here? I don't mean how have the stories been suppressed for so long, answers to which have emerged in numbers almost as profuse as the stories themselves. Rather, I'm asking what cultural conditions have led to such rampant, often perverted actions that not only subjugate people with little power, but testify to the warped vision of sexuality harbored by so many Americans? What possesses Charlie Rose to walk out of the shower and expose himself to a female assistant in his hotel room or to call her about his fantasies of watching her swim naked in the pool on his waterfront estate? Such distorted acts, of which countless examples exist, stem from something more than the abuse of power and privilege.

> **He is a classic sexual pervert, a man whose libido is so displaced that ... he recognizes none of Claudio's sensuality in himself, but, once he encounters a would-be nun, is undone by his own urges**

I'd speculate that *Measure for Measure* yields a clue about this mystery in the ironically named Angelo. He is a classic sexual pervert, a man whose libido is so displaced that, as the play opens, he recognizes none of Claudio's sensuality in himself, but, once he encounters a would-be nun, is undone by his own urges. Fashioning a fully rounded character of Angelo, Shakespeare endows him with the self-awareness to discern the strange dissonance between his lack of interest in available women and his passion for a woman whose spiritual purity and aspirations put her out of reach. 'What dost thou? or what art thou, Angelo?' he asks himself in a soliloquy. 'Dost thou desire her foully for those things / That make her good?' Not quite willing to own up to his responsibility in the matter, he first blames the devil for using one 'saint' – Isabella – to catch another – himself – then imagines Isabella as having irresistible power over him.

> Never could the strumpet,
> With all her double vigor, art and nature,
> Once stir my temper; but this virtuous maid
> Subdues me quite. Ever till now,
> When men were fond, I smil'd and wond'red how.

Angelo's twisted sexuality stands out even in *Measure for Measure*'s Vienna, where bawdy houses thrive and where the Duke says he's long 'seen corruption boil and bubble.' The city's licentiousness qualifies, in Renaissance terms, as unnatural; it breeds not children, like Claudio's natural, domestic union with Juliet, but venereal disease. Angelo's abrupt switch from absolute abstinence to sexual plundering, a shift that leads him to consider (and eventually to attempt) killing Claudio, is unnatural in the extreme. Angelo, of whom it is said that, 'when he makes water his urine is congeal'd ice,' shape-shifts into a criminal ruled by lust, and *Measure for Measure* gestures toward what has gripped Angelo, who 'scarce confesses / That his blood flows': his Puritanism. The sexual repression that Puritanism engenders, when ruptured, gives way to actions warped by long repression. That Puritanism is as much our own cultural inheritance as it is a direct influence over Shakespeare's Angelo.

Shakespeare and his contemporary playwrights

had every reason to despise Puritans. Collectively, they were kill-joys who wanted the theaters shut down for hosting decadent displays that misled youth and played havoc with an audience's senses. Plays were deemed fountains of temptation. Most threatening was the Elizabethan stage convention of cross-gendered casting, by which prepubescent boys played women's roles. Puritan warnings against such an ungodly practice took cross-dressing as formative; boys who played women, Puritans believed, could spontaneously become transgendered, forfeiting the sex traits that nature had given them. In 1642, the Puritans finally got their way; they closed down and eventually destroyed London's theaters, whipped persistent actors, and fined wayward audience members.

Angelo, as a state official, would have worn suggestively stiff clothes, particularly a rigid white collar, or ruff. His legal precision in sentencing offenders is of a piece with his implied Puritanism, as is at least one of several plays on his name. An angel was a coin whose image was stamped upon its exterior and was therefore superficial, skin-deep, like Angelo's virtue. Angelo's hypocritical extortion of Isabella under the guise of an upright judge and a public figure who styles himself above reproach matches the ironic discrepancy between outward sanctity and interior iniquity. It also translates almost seamlessly into our current social climate, abounding in figures, many of them churchmen and some of them judges, whose reputations for integrity and whose positions as role-models amount to only so much patina.

From the time religious protesters crossed the ocean, the sheer image of goodness, at odds with the deeper reality of decadence, has plagued their respectability. The seventeenth-century English poet Andrew Marvell, a decided Puritan and follower of Oliver Cromwell, wrote slyly ironic verses about the religious zealots who, referring to themselves as 'saints,' migrated to the Americas in smug assurance of their own spiritual election. To read about America's Founding Fathers, made prominent lately by interest in the musical *Hamilton*, is to be disabused of their rectitude and to discover sexual exploitation run amok. Although Alexander Hamilton himself was neither a Puritan nor a British immigrant, his appetite for women was legendary throughout his life, and his absorption in Maria Reynolds virtually ruined his political prospects. Thomas Jefferson's predilections included a host of married women and his household slave Sally Hemings. Aaron Burr gave full rein to his sexual voracity; he even bragged about his exploits repeatedly in letters to his daughter, Theodosia. In keeping with Puritanical hypocrisy, all of these political leaders gambled for power by excoriating one another's sexual breaches in writing without acknowledging their own.

At the core of American culture abides a friction between the mask of righteousness and the dark, hidden recesses of desire that elude understanding and self-control and that, released by virtue of power over others, render sexuality monstrous and perilous. Europe sees this paradigm – call it

Angelo's syndrome – and ridicules us for prudes. At the same time, the U.S. has been named the tenth most dangerous country for women and is the only western country on the list. The religious right, discounting sexual pleasure and disallowing any but heterosexual, reproductive intercourse, promotes abstinence-only programs that often backfire, presenting responsible non-abstinence as the better choice for young people. Where natural sexuality in all its forms is forbidden or seen as dirty, it will, like Angelo's, become deformed. It will smother the complaints of the injured, charging them with exaggeration and lying.

In *Measure for Measure*, to borrow the play's language, 'a remedy presents itself.' The characters' sexual looseness and deviance notwithstanding, the play is ultimately about sexual health, found between two committed people who love each other. It's really that straightforward. The model of such health in Shakespeare's play is the union between Claudio and Juliet, his pregnant fiancée. They are contrasted with the likes of Angelo, the Duke, Isabella, and many others, whose sexuality warps, to varying degrees, toward fear, repression and awkwardness. While the exemplary couple at the center of the play are heterosexual, and while the fruit of their love is a child, the fine details of their relationship aren't crucial. That Claudio and Juliet are not officially married suggests the possibility of a genuine love irrespective of legal and earthly trappings, and their unborn child symbolizes what truly distinguishes them: a mutual engagement with each other that cultivates and nurtures life. Juliet is listed under 'the names of all the actors' as the 'beloved of Claudio.' What matters is the 'beloved.' It's universally available, and although – despite the term's graceful simplicity – it is a long reach in our current polluted climate, it offers a way through. ◨

Notes

page 87. *'Sign me a present pardon for my brother…'*
All references to Shakespeare are from *The Riverside Shakespeare*, ed. G. Blakemore Evans and J. J. M. Tobin, 2nd ed., Houghton Mifflin, 1997.

page 95. Rolling Stone *debacle*.
In November 2014, *Rolling Stone* published Sabrina Erdely's article, "A Rape on Campus," which detailed University of Virginia student Jackie Coakley's gang rape at a Phi Kappa Psi fraternity party. After an investigation by the Charlottesville Police Department in January 2015 found no evidence to substantiate the article's claims, *Rolling Stone* retracted the article in April 2015. *Rolling Stone* details the journalistic short comings of the article in "Rolling Stone and UVA: The Columbia University Graduate School of Journalism Report: An anatomy of a journalistic failure." (Coronel et al.) https://www.rollingstone.com/culture/culture-news/rolling-stone-and-uva-the-columbia-university-graduate-school-of-journalism-report-44930/

page 96. *Judith Levine*, "Will Feminism's Past Mistakes Haunt #MeToo?" *Boston Review*, 8 Dec. 2017. http://bostonreview.net/gender-sexuality/judith-levine-will-feminisms-past-mistakes-haunt-metoo

page 96. *Masha Gessen*, 'When Does a Watershed Become a Sex Panic?' *The New Yorker*, 14 Nov. 2017. https://www.newyorker.com/news/our-columnists/when-does-a-watershed-become-a-sex-panic

page 97. *Jane Mayer*, "The Case of Al Franken," *The New Yorker*, 22 July 2019, pp. 30-45.

page 98. *The recent complaint lodged publicly against comedian Aziz Ansari.*
In January 2018, *Babe* published an article about an alleged sexual encounter between actor-comedian Aziz Ansari and a young woman who qualified their encounter as sexual assault. In the thick of the #MeToo movement and cancel culture, Ansari's reputation took a major blow until his statement and other news sources evaluated the claim to be little more than a disappointing sexual experience.
See Flanagan, Caitlin. "The Humiliation of Aziz Ansari." The Atlantic, 14 Jan. 2018. https://www.theatlantic.com/entertainment/archive/2018/01/the-humiliation-of-aziz-ansari/550541/

page 99. *(In June 2018, Judge Persky was recalled from office….)*
Maggie Astor. "California Voters Remove Judge Aaron Persky, Who Gave a 6-Month Sentence for Sexual Assault." *The New York Times*, 6 June 2018.

page 99. *He posted this limerick.*
Original investigation published by Minnesota Public Radio:
Euan Kerr, Laura Yuen, and Matt Sepic. "Investigation: For some who lived it, Keillor's world wasn't funny." *MPR News*, 23 January 2018. https://www.mprnews.org/story/2018/01/23/keillor-workplace

page 101. *Anne McClintock, professor of gender and sexuality studies at Princeton* McClintock is the A. Barton Hepburn Professor of Gender and Sexuality Studies, Affiliated Faculty: Princeton Environmental Institute and Department of English. https://gss.princeton.edu/anne-mcclintock

The Paris Pageant

by B. W. Jackson

One trip to Paris merges with the next.
At Charles de Gaulle, I nervously lay out my tattered
French to the woman behind the glass before hauling
my luggage through the turnstiles and down to the
platform. I slide into a seat on the commuter train,
plagued by doubts induced by a sleepless flight.
A Roma woman patrols the aisles between stops,
handing out notes with French on one side and
English on the other. Teenagers with headphones
and colorful backpacks gaze out the windows.

   After traversing the drab neighborhoods of the
banlieue, we go underground, and the seats fill up
around me. Paris seems to be crowding onto the
train. It isn't the Paris of my high school education,
populated by Philosophes and Sans-culottes.
The new Paris is diverse and scattered, yet still
avant-garde. The city is no longer the home of the
Impressionists, but the city itself has developed into
an Impressionist painting, colorful and fragmented.

I meet my sister at her classroom. She teaches
English and at present tutors an assortment
of illustrious Saudi wives, who tell her there is
nothing to do in Paris but buy purses and perfume

in between facials and manicures. Occasionally they look after their kids for sport. Otherwise they are touring the Champs Élysées, forming a new class of conspicuously consuming Parisians. More welcoming than the locals, they have become my sister's better companions. If only Balzac were around to dissect them.

She also has male students from Saudi Arabia, who are enthusiastic about their friendship with a liberated Western woman, complete with blonde hair and blue eyes. All of them are married and show no signs of romantic interest. A friendship with a woman seems to be exotic and daring enough to satisfy them. Back home in Saudi Arabia, an innocent trip out to dinner with a woman would be frowned upon, or far worse, in certain parts of the country.

Her friend and former student Saad, who works in security at the Saudi embassy, picks us up one evening for dinner. We drive in search of a restaurant, illegally traversing side streets in the vicinity of Rue Mouffetard as he entertains us with his broken phrases. With the help of my sister's English-to-English translation, I learn about his road to Paris. Saad grew up in rural Saudi Arabia and eventually found his way into a government security job in Riyadh. From there he transferred to the embassy in France. He is coming to the end of his stint and will soon return home, where no one will believe him when he describes his current existence.

After circling the same few blocks for twenty minutes, Saad remembers a restaurant on

Boulevard Saint-Germain, owned by an Italian-speaking Syrian married to a French woman. The restaurant serves as something of a refuge for Middle Easterners, and the owner readily offers Saad use of his basement for evening prayer.

Toward the end of dinner, the owner sits down with us, and soon we're engaged in a vibrant discussion of the Syrian civil war. He has clear ideas about what is happening, but little hope for resolution. In between points, he soberly shows us pictures of his war-torn home on his phone. My sister and I listen intently to his story, while curious French diners, suddenly foreigners in their own country, steal glances at us.

My sister and I listen intently to his story, while curious French diners, suddenly foreigners in their own country, steal glances at us

After dinner, Saad takes us on a roundabout route home. We can't tell if he is showing us the sights or if he is lost, but we enjoy the short tour. He is distracted by the radio, flipping through songs to give us a taste of Saudi music. We appreciatively bob along to the upbeat tunes, and he tells us the singer is 'Rashed'. The pronunciation is improbable. We break down in laughter. Rollicking in the backseat, I ask him to repeat it. 'Rashed', he assures me. Now I can't stop laughing. 'Raw shit?' I exclaim in disbelief.

As my laughter subsides, he turns onto a street that runs along the Seine. Across the river appears Notre Dame, glowing and ominous in the late evening.

Absorbed by the grand cathedral, I stare silently out the window as the music fades into the background. The play of light and shadow on the flying buttresses and stained glass captures all my attention and sends me plummeting into my thoughts.

The view is spellbinding, and yet the cathedral is unmistakably out of place. This old symbol of the city – this monolithic structure paying homage to a unified culture – no longer fits. I realize that Notre Dame is no more than a relic, an empty anachronism, the cathedral as beautiful, as cold as a mountain. In my stupor, we pass Shakespeare and Company on the left and Notre Dame disappears behind us. Meanwhile, the Saudi soundtrack plays on.

I am visiting Paris for the fourth time, and still I haven't been to Chartres. In the past, that would have been impossible. No American visited Paris without seeing Chartres. As the story goes, they would disembark at Le Havre and take a diligence through the countryside to Paris, stopping along the way to see the cathedral at Rouen. Then some time after that they would inevitably saddle up the horses and head south-west to Chartres.

A horse-drawn carriage might have been fun for a few miles, but I'm content to take the train, provided I can find the station. Leaving first thing in the morning, I get lost amidst the bending streets of Montparnasse and miss my departure. Boiling, I wander back outside to search in vain for a grocery store where I can buy materials for a picnic lunch. The workday is only just beginning. Commuters are still hustling to their offices. At a café next to the station, a middle-aged man and a young Vietnamese woman are putting on a demonstration of a lover's farewell, nearly tumbling out of their chairs in the process. They can't stop kissing and groping, and I can't stop staring.

By the time the next train departs, it is nearly mid-morning. Rush hour is over. The passengers board calmly. Before long, SNCF conductors saunter down the aisles inspecting tickets. Just ahead of me, a man and woman of African extraction fail to produce theirs, resulting in a fine. They explode in angry protest, causing the red-faced SNCF woman to retreat. But their victory is short-lived. She returns with a more imposing colleague who has no sympathy for their indignation. He shakes his head and blinks slowly with that imperturbable French insouciance that can be a pleasure to observe from a distance.

I open a book on my lap before taking a moment to count my money. I wonder what I'll do for a cheap lunch. When we arrive, I quickly discover that I need not have worried. Between the station and the cathedral there is not one but three kebab shops. I'll be able to check off another item on my list. Eating mystery meat carved from a glistening, rotating spit is as ceremonial for me as munching a baguette on the grass in front of the Eiffel Tower.

Approaching the church, I slow my steps, reminding myself that one only sees something for the first time once. I emerge out of the tight streets onto the square. The cathedral rises up before me, akin to a projection, or an optical illusion: a monumental toy block set down whole upon the earth. Delaying, I sit down on a bench in the back of the square and gradually come to terms with the immediacy of the structure.

Similar to Notre Dame, Chartres is somehow lifeless, despite its unassailable awesomeness. It is a temple once dedicated to God, but which now celebrates Man

I start my tour by exploring the outside of the cathedral, pausing to examine the details on the buttresses and within the portals. The dampness of the air and the heavy cloud creates a medieval effect, allowing me to indulge in a sense of mystery as I wander the grounds. The weather, too, has gone back in time. Peering up into the bell tower and the ramparts, I imagine that some ancient monk, some man of the Middle Ages preserved by magic, will appear and look down at me.

As I enter the cathedral, I can't help but think of all the distinguished figures who have made this same cultural pilgrimage. How many great minds and famous personalities have marveled and reflected as they ran a hand over these cold, worn stones? I hope that a profound insight will come to me, but I am too mired in admiration for the giants who have come before.

Similar to Notre Dame, Chartres is somehow lifeless, despite its unassailable awesomeness. It is a temple once dedicated to God, but which now celebrates Man. The spirit that once dwelt there has ascended. We now assume that medieval religion was no more than a unifying idea at best, and so we are incapable of getting beyond the ingenuity and wherewithal of the builders. We look at the stained glass and see the story of our predecessors' creativity; the soaring columns, intended to lift our heads to the heavens, take us only as far as the ribbed vaults. In an age without the divine, we are in danger of limiting ourselves to the confines of human reason.

Back in Paris, I meet my sister at Les Deux Magots, the old home to chic intellectuals. We thought we might sit down for a drink and indulge in a round of hagiography, but we are both put off by the scene. At the outdoor tables, fops in bright pants and unbuttoned collars are on display like dandelions. Women in big sun hats and still-bigger sunglasses surreptitiously evaluate one another. In more ways than one, it is another monument to human achievement, only much less captivating than Chartres.

At Les Deux Magots, and most other Parisian cafés, the outdoor chairs and tables face the sidewalk, as if seats in a theatre ... They aren't watching the spectacle, they are the spectacle

At Les Deux Magots, and most other Parisian cafés, the outdoor chairs and tables face the sidewalk, as if seats in a theatre. The guests sip their drinks and watch the people go by, perhaps unaware of the irony. After all, the guests are the ones on stage. They aren't watching the spectacle, they are the spectacle. Of course, for some, the only pleasure greater than having a tipple in honor of Hemingway at Les Deux Magots is being seen having a tipple in honor of Hemingway at Les Deux Magots.

Wavering, my sister and I decide to move on, neither of us anxious to crowd in among the other tourists. We were taught to be suspicious of what is popular. We associate nobility and class with inconspicuousness. Our understanding of a gentleman or a lady is one who is usually out of sight. The way to distinguish oneself is to be a person of distinction who appears indistinguishable. We aren't entirely above the allure of Les Deux Magots, but we are poor, and so we look for a place where we can get more for our money.

The day before my flight, I go out for a final stroll in the crisp air of early April. The trees along the boulevard are beginning to show green, and soon the tourists will arrive in droves. As the sun warms my face, pedestrians stream past, swirling around me like currents on a river. Cars and taxis and buses race in every direction, speeding toward their destinations. All this movement reinforces the joy of having nowhere to be.

Heading back to my sister's flat, I run into a crowd of French teenagers. An older woman is herding them along the narrow sidewalks in search of one site or another. She stops me to ask for directions, but quickly realizes her blunder when she sees my baffled smirk. The teenagers enjoy the gaff, and we laugh together as they file past. I can't deny the satisfaction of being mistaken for a native, even if by a discombobulated teacher presumably from some rural district of France.

Now I have played my small role in the Paris pageant. Saudi men give tours, Vietnamese women make love in cafés, Africans battle the SNCF, and the French ask Americans for directions. The French Foreign Legion has conquered the capital; France's captives have taken France captive. The only question that remains is how the captors will govern their territory. Today's Paris isn't the Paris of the French Revolution, but the revolution lives on, as they promised it would. ⊞

CREATIVE WRITING COURSES AND RETREATS 2020

WORKSHOPS • ONE-TO-ONE TUTORIALS • TIME AND SPACE TO WRITE

TUTORS INCLUDE:
Raymond Antrobus
Diana Evans
Mark Haddon
Willy Russell
Liz Berry
Nikesh Shukla
Paul Farley

GENRES INCLUDE:
Fiction, Poetry,
Non-Fiction, Theatre,
Starting to Write,
Children & YA,
Screenwriting

**Book now at
arvon.org**

LOTTERY FUNDED

Supported using public funding by
**ARTS COUNCIL
ENGLAND**

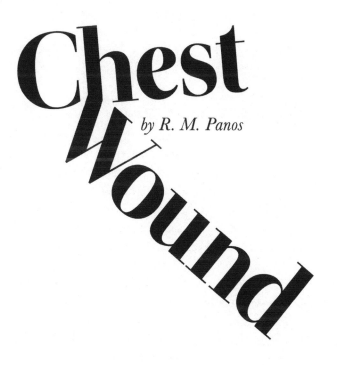

Chest Wound

by R. M. Panos

They called it the Miracle on the Hudson. The world applauded Captain Chesley Sullenberger's skill and cool head. Safely setting down a stricken Airbus 320 on the Hudson River required both. When asked how he accomplished the feat, Captain Sullenberger replied modestly, 'I was trained for it.' The sage comment evoked in me a vivid image. I knew how he felt, tension sweeping through my body at the advent of danger then easing as my entire being refocused to search for answers and actions.

Sullenberger's epiphany occurred while he held the controls of a crippled airplane. Mine came with my hands wrapped around a beating heart. It happened late one evening in 1990, four years into a five-year residency program at the US Air Force's Wilford Hall Medical Center in San Antonio.

The evening began as any other. I sat in loose scrubs, alone in the trauma center break room with a cup of coffee and a newspaper. The clock showed nearly midnight, about halfway through my 36-hour shift. The junior resident, Jim Carson, and I were in attendance, along with two interns, a crew of nurses, a few custodial staff, and a hospital full of patients.

Then Juan showed up, quietly deposited in a waiting room chair by his quickly disappearing compañeros. I didn't see him until he'd been installed in the trauma center's only fully equipped treatment room. Our young corpsman had already set up a fluid IV, and they were cutting away Juan's blood-soaked shirt. The tattoos on his body announced membership in a local barrio gang.

A tacit understanding stood between the barrio gangs and the trauma center staff: if they brought us their wounded, we would patch them up, ask no questions, and the San Antonio Police Department would not get involved until the next day. It worked, but years of peaceful co-operation had still not succeeded in persuading gang members to stick around. The only person who could reveal anything about what had happened lay bleeding on the examination table in front of me.

As his shirt came completely off, his status changed. 'GSW! Get a second IV in place.' My own handiwork in the shape of a midline abdominal scar evoked memories of a previous visit. I had seen him before. 'Juan, right?'

'Hey Doc,' he said low and labored. 'Wish I could say it was good to see you again.'

'What happened, Juan?'

Juan and his compañeros ran their operation under a strict code of conduct. Under that code, men in the barrio settled serious differences face-to-face, with knives, not guns. The code also allowed the barrio gangs to view the staff of the Wilford Hall Trauma Center as *servicemen*, much like themselves, which fostered an atmosphere of mutual respect. The apparent GSW – gunshot wound – announced something unusual.

'Take care of me, Doc. I was just minding my business when this dude shot me.'

A clean, small-caliber penetration just left of midline and above Juan's left nipple was bleeding somewhat less than one might expect. Juan seemed calm and in possession of his faculties. I wanted to know more about that bullet.

To call barrio men 'tough' does not do them justice and Juan's barely uttered groan told me the motion came with a good degree of pain

'Sorry, Juan, but I'm going to have to roll you over.'

To call barrio men 'tough' does not do them justice and Juan's barely uttered groan told me the motion came with a good degree of pain. Most people would complain in more graphic terms. Moving him only as much as necessary, I grabbed a look at his back. There it was, a neat little exit wound. What must have been a jacketed bullet had gone straight through Juan's body, hitting nothing hard and leaving behind no worrisome foreign objects. At the same time, the trajectory looked quite close to his heart.

Gently rolling Juan back, I glanced at the monitor, noting vital signs: Blood pressure, 70/50 – low, Pulse, 60 – low. Something didn't add up. Blood loss and the onset of shock should have invoked some tachycardia. His pulse should have been higher.

'How're you doing, Juan?'

'I don't know, Doc. I'm beginning to feel a little...' Before Juan could complete the thought, his eyes closed. A slur in his words sent my eyes again toward the monitor. No blood pressure at all. Distended veins along his neck spoke volumes.

My own heart went into overdrive. Hard truth seized the breath in my lungs. Juan had just fallen off a cliff and I knew he would die right there in front of me in a matter of seconds. My chest tightened and adrenaline surged through my veins. *Panic will not help.* Only a clear head could stand between Juan and death. Reaching past rising fear, I sought refuge in dispassion, desperately seeking answers among the fruits of my few years of training. The room became still and, as suddenly as it had come, the panic receded. In one long, frozen moment I realized what needed to be done. I stepped back and took a breath.

'We gotta open this guy's chest right now. Prep him for an ER thoracotomy and call Jim! STAT!'

As though visited by supernatural vision, I saw Juan's killer: something had a hold on his heart. The medical book would call it 'cardiac tamponade.' We needed to get at it. We needed to open his chest.

I became one of several intensely focused people. No time to scrub Juan clean. Without further instruction, our young corpsman opened a bottle of Betadine and poured its contents over Juan's chest, spreading the orange fluid to sterilize the skin as far around the wound as his hands could reach. A sweet hint of iodine mingled with the odor of blood and alcohol.

A junior nurse helped me into a pair of sterile gloves and tied a surgical mask around my face. The duty nurse, Lieutenant Christine Ellis, rolled the instrument stand near, laid out a surgical kit, and set a scalpel in my hand. The familiar dance fed the calm spreading in my head.

Like a priest celebrating Mass, I stood with hands raised searching for guidance, finding little to draw upon. The few chests I had opened before had all come to the trauma center free of vital signs – essentially DOA. Never before had I opened the chest of a living, breathing patient. *The first step will be the same.*

I made an incision just above the fourth or fifth rib; I would normally know exactly where that scalpel entered Juan's thorax, but here I didn't take time to count and the difference was not that important. Juan's heart needed space to beat. In one long motion, I drew the scalpel from the midline all the way down Juan's left side to the table. The incision began to seep, but Juan's low blood pressure kept the flow down. A second pass took me through the intercostal muscles and I looked into Juan's thorax.

The obstruction threatening Juan's life still lay hidden and the small space left little room for diagnosis, so out came the rib spreaders. Cranking as fast as I could, I opened the incision and didn't pause until Juan's ribs sent a sharp 'crack' across the room. The sudden fracture of two ribs pulled a gasp from more than one seasoned professional and nearly broke my clinical concentration. Juan did not seem to feel it and the shock quickly passed.

Peering inside, I saw the reason for Juan's struggle. Blood should have been flowing from the bullet hole in a bulging pericardium sac, but none did. Grabbing a pair of scissors from the instrument table, I cut. A mass of heart-stopping clotted blood forced its way out. Wasting no time, I reached in, scooped the dark mass into one hand, and turned to find Christine's hands holding a stainless steel pan waiting to receive it.

In the time required to tie even a single stitch, he would die ... I took the only course available and inserted one index finger into each hole

With the huge clot removed, Juan's heartbeat strengthened and I had time to further assess his condition. He was still alive, but barely. His heart still beat, but weak and slow. Blood flowed from the small hole visible in his right ventricle, but not as it should have done. The ventricle was not filling. I reached again into his chest to gently lift the heart, exposing a second stream of blood. The bullet had penetrated both ventricles! That Juan managed to keep breathing will forever amaze me.

Until both those holes were closed, there was nothing I could do to prevent Juan's imminent death. In the time required to tie even a single stitch, he would die. That simple fact left few options. I took the only course available and inserted one index finger into each hole. The bleeding stopped and Juan kept on living.

For what seemed an eternity I stood with Juan's slowly beating heart in my hands, unable to move and unable to do anything more to save his life. The room became a frozen tapestry of burgundy-colored scrubs and stainless steel furnishings, accented by the click of heels against a hard linoleum floor, and etched by the smell of blood and Betadine.

For what seemed an eternity I stood with Juan's slowly beating heart in my hands, unable to move and unable to do anything more to save his life

I felt at ease, knowing that Juan still lived and I had done everything possible to keep him so. He and I became one, a symbiotic pair. My hands kept him alive and his beating heart fed a quiet calm into my soul. At the same time, neither of us could stay that way for long.

The room released a collective sigh of relief.

About that time Jim showed up with George Santos, one of our anesthesiologists. Christine's anticipation had scored another point. Immobile and helpless, I could only nod. The room went on working. George inserted an endotracheal tube and began easing more air into Juan's lungs while O-negative blood flowed into his arm. Juan's heart began to fill and beat stronger. Hope began to replace the room's anxiety of only moments before.

But Juan's journey back into the land of the living would not progress far with my fingers stuck in his heart.

Jim stood by ready to help. For an instant, I considered the idea of holding my hands in place and keeping Juan's heart safely sealed while Jim stitched the two holes closed. Staring into eager eyes, I pulled everything I knew about him into my head. With only a single year of internship under his belt, I wondered how many types of stitches he had ever tied on living patients. I knew he could probably do it, but I also knew without a doubt that I could. We had to get this one right on the first pass. There would be no second chance. In no time I realized I needed to free at least one hand.

'Jim, can you get a finger into this left-ventricle hole?'

'Whenever you're ready.'

One careful little dance later, Jim and I were ready to swap fingers. After an exchange of nods and yet another deep breath, I pulled my finger from the hole in Juan's heart. Blood sprayed everywhere. The blood pressure we had diligently restored sent forth a powerful torrent. By the time Jim managed to get his finger into the hole, the two of us were soaked. Looking at my blood-covered colleague, I had to hope that Juan's worries did not include HIV.

With a free right hand, I then began to stitch around my left index finger, still buried in Juan's chest. The whole procedure became a mental exercise. My few years of real experience came back to guide every move, letting me clearly visualize how I must seal Juan's heart. I could see exactly how I should place stitches around my finger and enable myself to pull the opening closed as I withdrew. I could even hear myself describe those stitches to the oversight committee that would inevitably review my actions. Minutes later, I slowly retracted the finger while gently pulling up on the middle stitch, all the while watching for signs of leakage. When none appeared, I exhaled. *It worked!*

The inverted second hole required a little more finesse, but Jim's help and my two free hands soon had Juan's heart beating steadily with aid from no one's finger.

At that moment, Juan's retreat from death's door seemed destined to continue. Jim and I stood back and gave each other a silent 'Well Done.' Approving nods came from everyone in the room; everyone, that is, except Juan. Covered in blood, he still lay upon the treatment table telling everyone by the gapping hole in his chest that we were not yet finished.

As I began to repair my rough assault on Juan's body, placing large braided nylon stitches around the ribs I had ruthlessly fractured only a short while before, I noticed the intent look on Jim's face. He wanted to close that wound. *And, how else will he gain the experience he needs?*

'You want to close?'

Needing little encouragement, Jim stepped in and spent the next several minutes knitting stitches and punching staples into Juan's chest. Interjecting pointers over his shoulder, I remembered when I had been in his shoes.

Juan went upstairs to recover in the ICU while I went home feeling quite grateful, for the skill in my hands and for the many hours of training and experience that had put it there.

And now, so many years later, as I read of Chesley Sullenberger's humble explanation for the

Miracle on the Hudson, I can see him stepping off the wing of his floating aircraft feeling that same gratitude and relief.

In his case, all one hundred and fifty five passengers and crew of US Air flight 1549 walked off the plane ahead of him. No one suffered injury. In my case, I remember Juan walking out of the hospital a month later, sporting a little more scar tissue and likely telling lurid tales of his victory over the grim reaper. I never did take the time to tell him of the role he played in my own life. I should have done.

In his case, all one hundred and fifty five passengers and crew of US Air flight 1549 walked off the plane ahead of him.

Six months after his discharge, I saw Juan again, lying dead from an abdominal wound made by a sharp knife that had severed his lower aorta. **H**

LOVE IS A DICK WITH WINGS

by Dominic Laing

In the prologue of *The Illustrated Man*, a short story collection by Ray Bradbury, the narrator encounters a traveler, covered in tattoos. The traveler, known as The Illustrated Man, works carnivals and freak-shows, but always loses his job because his tattoos, or 'illustrations', have a life of their own.

> The pictures were moving, each in its turn, each for a brief minute or two. There in the moonlight, with the tiny tinkling thoughts and distant sea voices, it seemed, each little drama was enacted. Whether it took an hour or three hours for the dramas to finish, it would be hard to say. I only know that I lay fascinated and did not move while the stars wheeled in the sky.

> It's Friday evening and I'm at the Landmark, a bar in Southeast Portland with outdoor seating, a food truck and two ongoing games of corn-hole. I'm here to meet up with Jared Hunter, a tattooist who works a block away from the Landmark, at New Rose Tattoo.

From a distance, Jared fits in lockstep with tattoo culture and style. He's an Illustrated Man, tattoos draping his arms and legs. He keeps a messy facial hair combo of goatee and sideburns, and his hair juts out from his near-omnipresent SeeSee Motorcycle Company hat, which sits low on his brow.

Coming closer, however, I notice his eyes seem to be aimed slightly downward. Speaking to him, I learn he's shier than he looks. He loves to joke, yes, and when he does, his voice pitches and rolls, and his hands follow suit, waving and conjuring. But when the conversation digs beneath the surface, when he speaks more sincerely, his hands fold and his voice softens, so much so that I have to lean in to hear him clearly amid dinner banter, drink orders, and street traffic.

When I ask Jared how many tattoos he has, he replies that it's easier to gauge his tattoos in terms of percentage, as in 'What percent of my body is covered in tattoos?' Jared estimates that seventy percent of his body is tattooed.

The Earth is seventy percent water, and Jared is seventy percent ink.

—

Originally from Phoenix, Arizona, Jared grew up drawing and painting, and attended Northern Arizona University in Flagstaff for graphic design.

'I had no fucking clue what I wanted to do with my life, but I knew I wanted to do something creative.' The longer he studied graphic design, however, the less inclined he was to waste his talents by churning out slick ads at some bland agency; promoting shit he didn't want, didn't need and didn't believe in.

Instead, the young Hunter found himself attracted to the arts of tattoo and piercing. In the mid-to-late 90s, most tattoo shops offered piercings, and vice versa. The two were, in Jared's words, like 'peanut butter and jelly.' By the end of college, Jared had become friends with an artist at Burlyfish, a local shop in Flagstaff. It seemed the perfect spot for Jared to apprentice.

Jared came armed with a portfolio of drawings to show, but he laughs as he recalls his presentation, 'I had this sketchbook that I'd been working in for the past two months while I was building up the courage to ask him. It was so, soooo bad. But I thought it was just gold.'

'Everybody's skin is different, and every part of the body is different. Everybody takes ink differently, and everybody heals differently'

Whatever misgivings about the portfolio, Jared was hired. He still holds on to the sketchbook, as a reminder of how far he's come.

'What I do now is that if I'm working with an apprentice or somebody who's having a hard time, I've been known to bring out that sketchbook and say, "Take a look at this. Even though you're just starting, you're already years ahead of me."'

Artists are always working within constraints, and tattoo artists are no different. For Jared and other artists like him, one of the most unpredictable and challenging elements is the very surface upon which they create their art: human skin.

'Everybody's skin is different, and every part of the body is different. Everybody takes ink differently, and everybody heals differently. You have to learn how to adapt to those differences by feel.' Jared equates the unpredictability of skin to another art form: painting. 'If you're a painter, painting all your life on one particular kind of canvas, you know your canvas. You get used to the pull of the canvas, the friction of your brush against it... Imagine, then, that every single time, the canvas is completely different. Every single time, the canvas changes.'

The modern tattoo wave includes both a return to traditional American tattoos (bold colors, thick black lines), as well as more unique approaches, including Scientific Illustrations, ultra-fine needlework, and even white-ink tattoos. Jared, however, cautions against of-the-moment styles, because people don't consider the aging process when it comes to tattoos.

'Your skin is not a piece of paper. It's analog. The tattoo grows with your body, and it's scar tissue. That's how a tattoo works – you create scar tissue and inject it with pigment at the same time, so that when it heals, it heals to that pigment. As you age, it spreads in your skin.'

Carrie and Erica, two co-workers of Jared's, join us at the table. Erica wraps her arms around Jared, who's seated, but he stands to return the hug. When he leaves for a moment to get another beer, both Carrie and Erica tell me how much I've lucked out to be interviewing Jared. 'He's one of the good ones,' says Erica.

New Rose is a primarily female-run tattoo shop – Carrie not only works at the shop, but owns it as well – and it stands in stark contrast to the traditionally male-centric tattoo culture.

'I've worked at a number of mostly male shops,' says Jared, 'and I've always been the odd man out. It's this kind of boys' club. And here I am, this artsy, effeminate guy – like, I don't look that way, but being a man raised by women (mother, two older sisters, and a grandmother), I'm more in touch with my emotions than your average guy is.

'We know when somebody's having a bad day, and we have that unconditional love for each other – we support one another. Everyone here knows the shit we have to deal with,' he adds, 'because it can be a tough job. It's mentally and physically exhausting.'

In giving a tattoo, Jared doesn't merely draw a pirate ship on a person's arm. First, working from a pre-approved outline that's applied to the skin via Thermal Fax (the same technology used to create projector transparencies back in the 70s and 80s), Jared holds the person's arm in a fixed position, using his own body as ballast and stabilization. He positions the tattoo recipient in a way that'll allow the most leverage and flexibility during the inking process. Depending on what and where he's inking, poses include the 'Lethal Injection' (recipient flat on their back), the 'Karate Kick' (recipient with one leg bent/extended outward) and the 'A.C. Slater', also known as the 'Cool Professor' (recipient sitting backward in a folding chair). Once the recipient's settled, Jared then finds a position for his own body that both stabilizes the recipient (in case they squirm during the tattoo) and allows for maximum comfort, or as much comfort as can be found during a procedure that ranges from one to three hours. Next, Jared stretches the recipient's skin, tight enough to allow for ease of injection, but not so tight so as to cause bruising. Then he picks up his liner needle, a single instrument actually composed of several microscopic needles soldered together. His preferred weapon of choice is the nine-liner (nine needles). With this, he'll create the tattoo's outline. Once finished with the outline, he'll switch to the shader tool, or mag. Unlike the liner, whose needles come to a single point, the needles on a mag are staggered. For example, a seven-mag is four needles on the bottom, three needles on top.

His preferred weapon of choice is the nine-liner (nine needles). With this, he'll create the tattoo's outline

'In terms of visual difference,' says Jared, 'the liner needle's like a pen, whereas a mag is like a paintbrush. So you get a wider gradient and it covers more area.'

In using liner and mag needles, Jared employs a coil-operated device that uses the same alternating current technology that found its origins in Alexander Graham Bell's rotary telephone. The liner needle recoils and injects ink at a rate of 140 times per second. Such rapid repetition creates noticeable heat, which is why Jared says that for the uninitiated, getting a tattoo feels like 'a cat scratching a sunburn.' That needle must be guided to the perfect subterranean spot on the human body: beneath the first layer of skin (cutaneous) and resting between the second (subcutaneous) and the third, fatty layer.

'Feel is the hardest thing to figure out in tattooing. It's almost like you're landing a plane on an aircraft carrier'

'It's such a controlled chaos sort of thing,' says Jared. 'You're damaging skin, but you don't want to damage it too much. If you don't do it with confidence and nail it the first time, if you're being too careful about it, you're actually doing more damage because you're going over it too many times.'

'Feel is the hardest thing to figure out in tattooing. It's almost like you're landing a plane on an aircraft carrier.' Jared mimics the sound of a jet coming in for approach. 'You have to come in… and just before you land, take off. I knew I'd got better when I learned how to feel that sweet spot — feeling it in the vibration of the skin.'

Throughout all of this hyper-focused, moderately painful and potentially dangerous procedure, Jared must also maintain a warm, convivial bedside manner. He must listen to the recipient's stories, calm them if they're nervous, and cater to their every need as much as possible – lest someone give

Jared or New Rose a bad Yelp review.

Sarcasm aside, mistakes happen. A blowout, where ink spreads to neighboring tissue, is the most common kind of mistake. Search for examples of a blowout (or don't), and you'll see what looks like permanent bruises on the skin. The beauty of a well-drawn tattoo is genuine, but the risks of a tattoo are, like the tattoo itself, ever-present.

So yes, mentally and physically exhausting.

'This shit is hard, and it takes a long time to be steady,' says Jared. The reality of what's involved with giving a tattoo is why working with people like Carrie and Erica – who not only know the highs and lows of the job, but also have your back when things go wrong – is imperative.

'It took me a number of years to find this place that fits me perfectly,' he says. 'New Rose is like family… it's exactly like family.'

—

For those considering their first tattoo, the process for parsing out the specifics can be distilled into three steps:

Step one is 'WHAT.'

What exactly do you want tattooed? This information, says Jared, is much harder to glean from a customer than one would suppose. He provides an example conversation of how it occasionally plays out, playing the roles of both tattooist (himself) and customer:

FADE IN:
NEW ROSE TATTOO — INT. DAY
A customer (male, mid-twenties) walks into the shop.
JARED (early forties), a scraggly yet affable tattoo artist,
approaches the customer. Jared smiles.
Jared: Hey man. Welcome to the shop. What're you
       thinking about doing today?
Customer: Tattoo.
Jared: (nods) OK... well, you're in the right place.
       Let's start there. What do you want the tattoo
       to be of?
Customer: On my arm.
Jared: 'K, so it's going on your arm. What do you
want to put on your arm?
Customer: Just black and gray.
Jared: Well, what do you want to be black and gray?
Customer: Well, just like line work and stuff.
Jared: OK... but when you put the lines together,
       what do they form?
FADE OUT.

    Jared takes a sip of his beer and shrugs. 'It's
the last thing people want to tell you. Just fucking
say, "I want a dick with wings." Alright! Now we
know what we're getting. Anything helps. Give me
specifics. "A scorpion wizard! On a jet ski!"' He
quiets for a moment, then smiles. 'Nobody ever says
"I want a dick with wings."'

    When I walked into New Rose for the first time
and sat down in the waiting area, I found myself
next to Halston Hoover, a young naval ensign

(pronounced 'in-sin') who looked like he had stepped right out of a recruitment poster: square jaw, blue eyes, crisp uniform, ramrod straight posture. He waited quietly, gazing down at the pages of a little black sketchbook.

'Are you getting a tattoo?' I ask him.

He nodded, enthusiastically. 'Yeah, first one.'

I pointed to the sketchbook. 'Is that it?'

He opened the sketchbook to me, and I saw a roaring lion's head with a tree-covered mountain as background. Stormy seas, tilting ship included, formed the mountain base. Within the sea was a Bible verse, Psalm 95:4-5: 'In his hands are the depths of the earth, and the mountain peaks belong to him. The sea is his, for he made it, and his hands formed the dry land.'

He quiets for a moment, then smiles. 'Nobody ever says "I want a dick with wings"'

The Navy has a long tradition with tattoos. During World War II, a man by the name of Norman Keith Collins tattooed many officers stationed in the South Pacific. These days, Collins goes by another name: Sailor Jerry. Although he might be more famous today for his rum than his tattoos, he established the American Traditional Style of Tattoo.

One of the recurring tattoos of that time, Halston told me, was that of pigs and chickens on the tops of sailors' feet. 'Back when they transported animals via ship, they kept the animals in wooden crates down below deck. If the ship sank, the crates of the animals would float, because they were made of wood. Having a pig on one foot and a rooster on the other was almost like having a good luck charm.

Step two for a tattoo is 'WHERE.'

'Sometimes placement dictates design,' said Jared. 'If you're doing it on the arm, that's a tall, vertical silhouette, whereas a chest, back, sometimes leg tattoo – that's more of a landscape thing.'

I watch as a customer named Charlie gets 'CEDRIC,' his second son's name, tattooed on the inside of his right bicep. The letters are a custom block font, a combination of the logos for The Incredible Hulk (cinderblocks, hard edges) and Teenage Mutant Ninja Turtles (turtle shells, curves, organic). His first son's name, 'KILLIAN', is on the inside of his right bicep.

Jared had to turn away a customer who wanted an unreasonable amount of detail ... 'She wanted thirty pounds of shit in a five pound bag'

With Charlie is his tatted-out wife, Debra. They're celebrating their third anniversary, and they've come from Gresham, a town that neighbors Portland, to get the tattoo. While Charlie's getting his tattoo, Debra's talking to Jared about potentially adding a Dementor from Harry Potter to her body of work. She's torn between her calf or the top of her thigh, but she can't make a firm decision yet.

People sometimes prank-call the shop and say they want to get tattoos on their genitals or genital area. Almost all of the time, nothing comes to fruition. But in Jared's case, one customer was no prank.

'I tattooed a taint once,' he said. 'A lot of guys call about getting tattoos on their dicks, but they never go through with it. This guy though, he was super-nice about the whole thing. He said he'd thought about it for a while and wanted to do it as a surprise for his partner.'

Jared respected the man's thoughtfulness about the situation, and though unorthodox in nature, he agreed to the man's request. The tattoo was done in two sessions. When completed, the tattoo read 'BAD BOY.'

'The funniest thing about the whole experience,' said Jared, 'was that I had to turn my hat backwards, because the brim of the hat kept hitting his junk.'

Step three, 'SIZE/DETAIL,' is most often determined by cost. The base price for a tattoo at New Rose hovers around $150. A cash deposit (and cash alone) that partially covers one's total payment is required before the tattoo is drawn. Recently, Jared had to turn away a customer who wanted an unreasonable amount of detail. Or, in his words, 'She wanted thirty pounds of shit in a five pound bag.'

'She had all this detail, but she wanted it to be the size of a quarter. She wanted a cat, lettering that said "Wish You Were Here", a banana tree, on and on. I drew it up for her, and it was yay big,' he said, holding up his palm. When she insisted on the tattoo being the size of a quarter, Jared politely, but firmly, suggested she find another tattooist.

'Just because you thought of it,' Jared says, 'doesn't mean it's possible. I don't go to my mechanic and tell him, "Hey, could you put a flux capacitor in my car so I can travel through time?" Because my mechanic'll say, "No, I can't do that." I'll tell him, "I've been thinking about this for years, that's how I want it." "Well I'm sorry sir," he'll say. "Time travel isn't possible."'

Aside from the questions of What/Where/Size and Detail, the obvious question concerning tattoos is 'WHY.'

For Halston, the naval ensign, it marks the next step in his career. He wants to get the tattoo before he ships out for Charleston, South Carolina, where he'll be attending Nuclear Power School. 'I've thought about it for a few months, and the idea finally settled in my mind.'

The image of the ship sailing through stormy waters speaks to both his life as a naval officer and his personal faith. 'We like to think of ourselves as indestructible,' says Halston, 'but we're all fragile, floating through life, and yet God owns the wind. In some ways, God's untamed and doesn't conform. But He's also gentle enough not to destroy a wooden ship.'

For Jared, he finds that the answer to 'Why do people get tattoos?' falls into two main categories: 'Time in your Life,' (army enlistment, college, etc.) and 'High Art' (angel wings, shields, flowers, etc).

'I like it when it's both a time in your life and high art,' he says. 'I have tattoos that I've spent months being into the symbolism of things, putting shit together, and then...' He pauses, and smiles. 'Well, OK. I had a dream once. It was the plot to *Say Anything* – the 1989 romantic drama starring

John Cusack, most famous for the scene where Cusack stands outside his girlfriend's house and raises a boom box playing Peter Gabriel's *In Your Eyes* above his head.' Jared continues, 'So, it was the plot to *Say Anything*, but it was set in the 1800s; Victorian-Era England. Everybody's in period garb – top hats, trench-coats and dresses. So, with the boom box scene, what do you think he had raised above his head?'

'I have tattoos that I've spent months being into the symbolism of things ... and then...' He pauses, and smiles

Jared pauses and waits for me to guess. When I can't come up with anything, he grins, like showing me the location to buried treasure. '...He had a gramophone.' Jared pulls back his left sleeve and shows me a perfectly outfitted Victorian gentleman, hoisting a gramophone high above his top-hat covered head.

At the base of the gentleman's feet is a ribbon, which reads 'In Your Eyes.'

—

For Jared, the joy he finds in his work as a tattooist stems not as much from the artistic element as it does the relational component.

'I love having conversations with people, how personal it all is. You'd be amazed the shit that people share at that point of vulnerability.'

In one sense, Jared's a hardened veteran of the

tattoo and piercing world. In another, he's a fount of gentleness and compassion, unexpected given both his profession and physical appearance.

He reminds me of Winnie the Pooh… if Winnie the Pooh also had gauged piercings, 'OLDE SOUL' inked on his knuckles and gave Eeyore discounted tattoos on Friday the 13th. But as it pertains to friendship, love and empathy, Jared's neck-and-neck with 'ole Pooh Bear.

He reminds me of Winnie the Pooh… if Winnie the Pooh also had gauged piercings, 'OLDE SOUL' inked on his knuckles

'I go on an emotional ride with people because sometimes, I feel like it makes it easier for them. Take a memorial tattoo, for example. This one lady had a son – sounded like a cool kid, an artist who was into recording – died at 17, 18. He crashed on a skateboard, cut his leg on a truck chassis, contracted this bacteria – killed him within a week. She was in the shop, telling me this story, and I had to stop 'cuz she's bawling, and I started tearing up too because it was so heavy and I needed a second.

'If you cry, chances are I'm going to cry too. I have a credo from Steel Magnolias – I think it was Dolly Parton. She said, "Nobody cries alone in my presence."'

Tattoos are proclamations, invitations, compass bearings, defense mechanisms, confessions and concealments. They're bets lost and dares acted upon. They're reckless and impulsive. They're careful and considerate. They're acts of defiance, resilience, grieving and celebration. They're a way of saying, 'This, this is the fire I walked through. This is the hell, and this is the high water. This, this is the joy that guides me. This, this is the love that sustains me.'

They're evidence of a life.

We all confront questions of who we are, how we are, and why we are. For many, tattoos are not only instrumental in discovering the answers to those identity questions, but in holding onto those answers as well. They're a physical manifestation of the sacraments nearest – and dearest – to us.

Let me sit and tell you about fire. Let me sit and tell you about light.

No one's alone in these explorations, revelations and anxieties. At times, it feels as if we're poring over a table full of fragments, potential evidence of something larger; something right in front of our noses, yet undiscerned at that moment.

Let me sit and tell you about water. Let me sit and tell you about blood.

If we lay out enough fragments, we think (and hope and pray), something will assemble. The disparate pieces will, as we are faithful, gather and unify into something greater – something whole.

Let me sit and tell you about grief. Let me sit and tell you about love.

We want a Virgil to our Dante, someone who walks with us into the dark and, hopefully, through it. Jared, if only for a few hours, plays Virgil to those walking through their personal Infernos, Purgatorios and Paradisos. He ingests, interprets and repeats their stories back to them in illustrated form.

Let me sit and be seen. Known. Your eyes in my eyes. My eyes in your eyes.

Enduring pain for the sake of remembrance – for the sake of something beautiful – and doing so with someone who hears your story and acknowledges you in all your fullness… that's communion. And communion is what we crave. We want to be assured that if we reach out, someone's going to reach back and grab hold of us. We want to know that when we fall, we make a sound – because someone heard us fall.

Jared, in word and deed, in presence and ink, is one who says, 'I hear you. I see you. And I'm with you.' **H**

The Royal Society of Literature

RSL Spring 2020 events include

Wednesday 19 February
6.30pm, London School of
Economics
Writers Rebel

Chloe Aridjis, A.L. Kennedy
and Daljit Nagra – all
members of the Writers Rebel
group who protested against
climate change discuss
whether such movements can
make a difference.

Monday 16 March
7pm, British Library
*What's So Great About
E.M. Forster?*

Deborah Levy, Laurence Scott
and Preti Taneja celebrate
Forster - one of Britain's most
esteemed novelists - 50 years
after his death.

Monday 11 May
7pm, British Library
Monstrous Women

Nimco Ali, Maggie Gee and
Laurie Penny explore what
happens when women fail
to meet the expectations of
society, and how literature
can confront monstrosity in
woman's form.

Friday 22 May
7pm, National Portrait Gallery
Dressing Up

Marking the Gallery's major
exhibition of Cecil Beaton's
work, Amrou Al-Kadhi and
Tom Rasmussen consider
dressing up, self-portraiture
and autobiographical writing.

**RSL Members can attend all events for free.
More information: rsliterature.org**

Deeper Than Than Blue

by Lily Bungay

Baby Matina sleeps in the cool of the living room.
 She's sprawled out on the sofa, drowsy from the heat. Her mother and grandmother are fussing in the kitchen, conversing almost inaudibly.
 Matina took her first steps this morning and they've decided to celebrate with cake.

A top layer of peach, the colour of honeycomb, balances on a sloping rectangle made of custard cream and chopped up biscuits.

Dappled light dances across the table and the cake glistens while I politely await the nod from Grandma to sit and eat.
 She nods.
 It's velvety, fluffy, delicious.

The cicadas have awoken. They fill the sea air
with their persistent chorus. I recede momentarily
into thoughts of my own childhood; my mother
describing how the sound of these insects would
flood her mind with charming memories of summer.

I look out over the hills, which are bathed in
afternoon light, and slowly inhale the view. This
is my favourite time of day, when the bakeries and

cafes have closed their doors and everyone in the
village is napping. I feel as though the entire island
is mine to explore.

This unassuming island in the Aegean Sea is Ikaria
(ee-kah-ree-ah). Its residents are known to live well
into their nineties and beyond. That's the reason
I'm here; the unhurried rhythms of the place.

Another hair-pin bend and I quickly glance at the bunches of grapes piled up on the passenger seat next to me.

Checking the plump little orbs are still firmly in place, I slow to a Sunday-driver pace and watch the scenes of island life pass by.

A pair of well-worn jeans and navy overalls slung over the branch of a tree, along with a plastic bag containing only a packet of cigarettes.

Figs laid out in rows across a table, drying in the sun.

An abandoned car with a sad face drawn into the dusty windscreen.

Back in the village.

Knock on the door. No response.

Knock a few more times.

Chairs scraping, then a slow pad towards the door. He appears, the kitchen behind him like a dark cave. A bear woken from a deep sleep.

This is Christos.

He wears a white vest stretched over his big belly, a matching white cap. The hairs on his arms and hands are bleached from the sun. He looks like Father Christmas. He takes me on a tour of his garden. He runs his hands through the tendrils of the vines as we meander past densely packed fruit trees and grapevines.

Pomegranate and ruby red apple trees, hefty marrows weighing heavily on the ground, cartoonish in their exaggerated colours and size.

Under the shade of an olive tree, I can't tell if he's still groggy from his siesta or just unimpressed with my questions.

'Are you really the strongest man in the village?' I ask.

'Yes. Up to this day I am considered the strongest. I've worked hard all my life. I've done the work 20 people would do in a lifetime.'

He shows me words written on the back of a child's drawing:

'My great-grandfather has the most beautiful garden. He is very handsome. He has white hair and he is never in a hurry.'

Windows down; the sweet, fresh smell of honey and pine everywhere. Powder blue bee hives flash their smiles from between the trees.

Tarmac turns to rocks the size of my fist. Matina's mother reassured me that this is a well-known route; I'm unconvinced. A barren, white-washed landscape, it makes me think of the Moon. Except, it's windy up here. Bells clanging from the goats which now surround me.

Nikos is coming.

He said to meet at 10am, but no one keeps time here. No one is ever on time; no one is ever late.

A packet of biscuits. A present for Nikos.

A banged up blue truck, blue overalls, and a faded blue cap. A warm smile and a grey handlebar moustache. Nikos is a goat farmer and restaurateur. He comes up here every morning to feed his goats and sometimes stays the night in his stone hut – when he wants a break from his wife, he tells me with a chuckle.

I step inside. There's a cupboard filled with whisky, a gun on the bed.

Nikos lights the camping stove and shortly after we are drinking coffee from tiny cups. It's thick and gritty. Looks like treacle, but tastes like something that might clog up your insides.

Nikos laughs. 'Why do you think we drink it in tiny cups?'

I open the packet of biscuits and eat one with every mouthful of coffee.

Another village. Another home.

On the kitchen floor, something blue catches my eye.

There's a clock on the wall, but I don't know if it tells the right time. Behind it a picture of a saint and two angels.

'I go to church, but I'm not a fanatic.' Everyone uses that line.

Aviera places a small bowl of porridge in front of me. We sit facing each other, smiling, eating our watery oats. For a moment we are in unison.

Blue apron. Garden shoes on. She climbs the steps
to the chicken coop, a bucket in each hand. A spray
of pellets, like gold dust as they catch the light.
Down on her hands and knees, the soles of her shoes
are caked in garden crumbs. Aviera shuffles inside
the brick-built hen house until her head, shoulders
and arms disappear. It reminds me of playing hide
and seek with an adult who, too big for a child's
den, can only fit their head inside. It's a fairytale
and she's a giant in the chickens' Lilliputian world.
She backs out, hands filled with treasure.

She wields the hose-pipe in one hand and in the
other, plucks sage and oregano leaves, handing
them to me, inviting me to inhale their scent. A
welcome gesture from one stranger to another.
I pause. Discarding the herbs seems careless, so
instead, I stuff them in my pocket and rub them
between my fingers.

I tilt my face towards the sky and feel the weight of my hair as it drinks in the water. I close my eyes. Alone in the sea. Alone on this island. But not lonely.

Later, in the pitch-black night, I follow the muffled sounds of stringed instruments and chatter down a steep path, into a courtyard. Lanterns criss-cross above a heaving dancefloor.

In unison, the people sway inwards, then back out again, like the bellows of the musician's accordion. I try to follow their footwork, to see if there is some kind of pattern. If there is, I can't make sense of it.

The musicians all wear the harried expression of someone who is about to miss a train. A voice sings an extended cry of joy, another whistles, the tempo increases excitedly, and they transition into a new song without pause.

I climb up on a wall and look out over the sea of
people, my head in a cloud of cigarette and cooking
smoke, illuminated by the lanterns above.

Two small friends chase each other through the
crowd. One escapes the other by hurtling towards
the throng, momentarily trapped. He weaves in and
out of hulking legs, which swing and kick in time,
and shoots out the opposite side of the dancefloor
and then launches himself into the lap of a jolly
grandparent.

I raise my camera to take a picture, catching the subtle scent of herbs still on my fingertips from Aviera's garden. I hesitate, watching through the viewfinder. The music never breaks, the dancing never stops. The laughter, the smiles and the energy never drop. For a brief moment I am lost in time. The island is alive, and I am witnessing its heart beating at full pace. Nobody can stop it. Except me.

Click.

Believe

by Ingrid Fagundez

I was introduced to God as I was introduced to sex, on the same dark night.

I went with my parents to a farmhouse. The road was dirty and dust filled our lungs. In my dreams about that day, there is an amusement park along the route, a roller coaster on the fields, but that is just a fantasy: there were only cows, fences and an orange dusk. The sun was almost setting when we arrived and I can picture us driving up the hills, climbing out of our grey Santana and saying hello to the hosts – friends of my dad. They leaned forward to stamp wet kisses on my cheek. How beautiful I am, they said.

The house was made of wood. It had a couple of bedrooms and all the doors were open. There were more people there, adults and kids, and a boy. A brown-haired, older, pretty boy who stared at me. I wanted to look at him but couldn't, something would pinch me on the chest when I did, and it felt good.

As night fell, the children ran around the house playing Catch One. The boy preferred Hide and Seek. He asked me to go for a walk with him, he knew the area, he was a neighbour. My mom said I could, so I went. The sky was crowded with stars arranged without logic – big, small, bright, almost fading, tight together in shining chaos. Despite their light, it was dark. The house got further and further away as we walked into the blackness, and I could sense it in my body, getting dense, cold, involving us.

I was scared when he asked if I knew the differences between boys and girls. No, I didn't. Boys have a thing in the middle of their legs; girls have a thing inside. Inside where? He kept explaining it and touched me. Do you want to grab it? I was unsure, I guess I didn't. In the distance, I could see a man approaching us, coming from a barn, in the opposite direction to the house. I took the opportunity and ran. When I found Mom having a drink on the balcony, I asked her if they were looking for us.

No, she answered, we're all here.

As I prepared to go to sleep that evening, I called her. I didn't understand what had happened, so the words would bump into my teeth and come out shattered. She listened for a minute. I don't remember her explanation but the voice was calm and low, unlike her normal tone. There was something about boys, pipis and being careful. She was intrigued by the man.

Where did he come from?

The barn, I said, in a red shirt.

Hm… There was nobody dressed like that.

Then she told me about seeing people that weren't there. It was common, she knew all about it. Things we cannot touch but still exist. The substance of things. Like God. She used to mention

Him all the time and I had heard about His deeds from the priest, but at seven years old I finally got it: God was a non-existent man in a red shirt.

These memories are fragmentary and blurry. I often don't trust them. But they carry the essential element to faith and love: mystery. And, sometimes, unreliability.

On Sundays, I prayed not to go to mass. It wasn't exactly a prayer, but a supplication.

Please, please, Mom, let us stay home today, I would say.

My mother is very Catholic, in her own way. She makes me and my sister carry little portraits of saints in our wallets and in the bottom of our suitcases for protection. During our childhood, she wanted to go to mass every week. It was her appointment with God, one we didn't want to attend.

Sundays were lazy days at home, in Florianópolis, an island in the south of Brazil. In the morning, Mom would take us to the park to ride our bicycles and walk the dog. The lawn was next to the ocean and we would watch the wind create little waves while sweating our bodies under the sun. The breeze was refreshing and comforting. It would bring promises of freedom, promises broken a while later, when we would return home not to leave again until Monday.

My sister and I would observe the afternoon dying outside while we played and fought and played a little more in our narrow apartment. We felt trapped. Mom wouldn't take us anywhere, she needed to rest, she said, and the streets were dangerous for kids. Dad worked on weekends, the computer an extension of his arms. There was only one way out: the church. But that was even worse than staying at home.

The stained glass windows filtered the light through images of Jesus' Calvary – red for the blood, blue for his pleading eyes

My church belonged to the Middle Ages. As a child, it never occurred to me that the institution no longer sold pieces of heaven or burnt books. Although I studied at a Catholic school, that did nothing to change my concept of Catholicism – my history teacher was really into marijuana and the persecution of heretics and forgot to explain what happened after the Renaissance. I also blame Umberto Eco's *The Name of the Rose*. The movie based on the novel, set in a 14th century filled with execution scenes, became a favourite; I watched it too many times. When Mom invited us to church, I imagined pain, fire, and decapitated bodies. I preferred TV.

The dark orange bricks and the small entrance door gave the central nave a gloomy atmosphere. The stained glass windows filtered the light through images of Jesus' Calvary – red for the blood, blue for his pleading eyes. We would sit on the benches in the back before the priest started rebuking us for our sins.

Our wrongdoings don't make us happy in eternity, he would say.

He usually looked sad, wrinkles on his forehead, a hard cast to his lips. As we listened to him talk about our guilt, old ladies would stare at us.

Why was my mom alone? Didn't she have a husband? They asked each other while praying.

Aren't Christians good people? I wondered while daydreaming.

My mother knew about the questions but tried to ignore them. I would fall asleep on her shoulder amidst the sermon and the gossip.

—

A man used to walk across our living room, wearing a top hat and a dark suit. He was always in a hurry. My sister and I never spotted the visitor, but there he was again, Mom said. She would cross herself after his appearances. She didn't believe in spirits, they didn't fit her Christian faith.

My mother never liked to discuss her visions. Last winter I was at my parents' house when she came in from the kitchen, after dropping something on the floor. I looked away from the TV when she started talking, a wet dishcloth on her shoulder, an absent expression on her face.

There was a lady with short hair there, when I was washing the dishes, she sighed. You see how things are...

And went back to cleaning.

The Bible is not very receptive to mediumship.

The writer of Leviticus (20:27) suggests that 'a man or a woman who is a medium or a necromancer shall surely be put to death. They shall be stoned with stones; their blood shall be upon them'.

But Mom is not in danger, she follows the rules. I'm the one who chooses a sinful path. I embrace God and take him on my spiritual *adventures*.

—

The autumn breeze makes the wind chime swing softly. Its tinkling is the only sound apart from the rustling trees. The white curtains blow behind me but the cards remain immobile. The fortune-teller places her hands on them.

> **But Mom is not in danger, she follows the rules. I'm the one who chooses a sinful path. I embrace God and take him on my spiritual *adventures***

What do you want to know?

I was there as a Journalism student with homework: a profiling exercise about an interesting character. Graça was more than interesting. Everything that she said – how the job worked, when she started and what were the voices in her head – sounded fascinating to me. After the interview she offered me a free tarot reading.

This is what I wrote in 2011: 'She sits across the table and starts telling me about her life, childhood, profession. Graça or Gracinha, as she was nicknamed by her father, is a 53-year-old fortune-teller. She doesn't bring the loved one back in three days or reveal the lottery numbers, but she assures me she can predict the future, disclose present secrets and retell past lives. These predictions, she explains, pop up inside her head, as part of her imagination. In contrast, her observations about the present and the past are based on images that appear on a type of immaterial screen behind every client.'

My then boyfriend had been my husband in a previous incarnation. He had died in a plane crash travelling to former Czechoslovakia

I couldn't read her properly – not then, not now. Her presence made me feel apprehensive and at ease at the same time. I was too young, small in my seat, trying to describe her when she had already deciphered me thoroughly. I didn't have enough eyes. She had them all.

Pick three cards, please, and give them to me.

To avoid my reflection in the mirror placed on a side wall, I stared at her. Black tank top straps and red bra loops, interlaced in a braid. She rubbed scented oil on her hands and then on mine, her long dirty nails scratching my palms lightly. The cards started to reveal themselves. The breeze and my expectations made me shiver.

I don't want to hear anything bad, I said. I'm very impressionable.

I know that.

Graça spoke about my parents' marriage and my mother's teenage years with precision. She even described how Mom used to dress.

I fancy her, Graça said, she looks like a gypsy, full of rings.

I was indeed impressed but didn't have time to analyze her techniques. Graça asked me to cut the cards in three piles, then she shuffled them again and laid some out on the table. She wanted to talk about my past.

My then boyfriend had been my husband in a previous incarnation. He had died in a plane crash travelling to former Czechoslovakia.

You were pregnant, she added.

The story had further details, but I don't recall them. As she continued, a dream catcher spun behind her head, caught by the wind, and its movement cast me back to 1940s Soviet Union. The communist soldiers, the tweed dresses, the blond kids on my lap...

Let's take a look at the future? Graça called me back.

My fingers were pressed against my thighs, blotting off the sweat. My mouth opened to refuse the offer – fearing that if I knew what was about to happen I would stick to these visions – but then, out of curiosity, I hesitated. I didn't need to know the future, but I wanted to.

Two great loves would come my way – *breathtaking* loves, Graça explained with a side smile. Nothing I had known up until then. It was not a boyfriend, but a man (or two), she emphasized, and I would have kids with one of them. And I would write books – yes – books about things like this, she said, pointing to the cards.

I don't see myself as a writer. Never did. But her prophecy finds a way to materialize itself in these pages, as I type down the words.

Look what I've found, Mom said, waving a green-covered book in the dim store.

The air smelled of aroma sticks and flowers and beside her, a miniature cauldron decorated a shelf.

I thought you might like it, she continued, handing me the book.

Tarotmania, by Jan Woudhuysen. That was all the information on the front cover, beside an amateurish drawing of a gypsy man. On the back, the advertising of other titles from the same publishing house: *The Paranormal, Space – Time and Beyond* and *The Reflexive Universe – Evolution of the Consciousness and The Geometry of Meaning.*

Where was it?

Right here, she pointed out. The tarot section.

We found the bookshop after a couple of hours at the British Museum. Mom was visiting me in the UK, where I was studying for my Masters, and since I had forgotten to plan the rest of the afternoon, we decided to go for a walk in the neighbourhood. When we saw 'The living history of magic' painted on the window of The Atlantis, we didn't need to discuss it. I entered the store and she followed me.

My idea was to locate titles about tarot. I was searching for them, lost between the astrology and the Wicca shelves, when mom's voice broke the ritualistic silence of the place. I hadn't told her the aim of my hunt.

How did you guess? I asked.

Well, I knew you like the subject… and maybe it

can help you understand, you know, the changes in life, she murmured while running her fingers across the spines of the paperbacks.

I left her flipping the pages of a numerology manual and stepped across the red Turkish rugs to the other side of the room. At a wooden table that served as the cash desk, two plump, middle-aged women chatted under the hard winter light. I opened the book and chose the chapter concerned with the meaning of the cards, looking for one specifically.

Look what I've found, Mom said, waving a green-covered book in the dim store. The air smelled of aroma sticks and flowers

'The Tower represents the fact that as our illusions are shattered we must grasp the opportunity to grow. That is why I asked the artist to show the Tower as a picture of two children totally engrossed in building their seaside fort. Only when Reality starts tearing up their picture do the children realize that all is an illusion. Will that knowledge drive them insane, or will they grasp the opportunity to make friends with the giant?'[1]

Will Reality drive them insane? I asked myself, examining the boy and the girl drawn on the old paper.

Jan Woudhuysen, the introduction said, had been studying the Tarot for five years when he decided to write about it, in 1979. For him, the practice was a method of self-development of the psyche. Rather than contacting the spiritual world, the goal would be to get in touch with one's subconscious, its hidden traumas and desires. There was a godly element to it, Woudhuysen admitted, but the most important thing was to recognize what the symbols meant to you.

Will you buy it? Mom asked, suddenly in front of me, her green eyes on the cover. They had the same mossy tone.

I think so.

As one of the women wrapped my purchase, the roses next to her exhaled a weak perfume. I touched the petals lightly before noticing Mom was analyzing me.

Will you buy it? Mom asked, suddenly in front of me, her green eyes on the cover. They had the same mossy tone.

You can try to see your future in love, she joked, her words knocking on my back.

Yeah, sure, I muttered.

I was already reading the cards, I almost told her before closing my mouth again. The lady gave me the brown package and smiled, her purple lips stretched on white skin. I was reading them every day, I thought, as we walked out the door, the package pressed against my chest, air stealing the heat from our bodies. I was reading them with my eyes closed, whispering, wishing, praying – seeking for an answer. I waited hungrily for the answer I desired to receive.

—

We sat behind the cemetery. The night was hot and windy and above us the buildings stretched through cloud, covering the sky. I looked up trying to count the surviving stars; he leaned towards me, lips slightly open, without a word. I turned aside. Horns and sirens filled our silence.

I had known Fernando for a few months, through work. He was just an acquaintance then, a stranger, a stranger I already loved. I fell for him in the absence of reason or time. My love just was; there, on the sidewalk.

Are you crazy? I asked.

One kiss, he said. Just one kiss.

No, I repeated, hiding my face with my hands.

He held them tight, with sweaty fingers. They fitted perfectly. It couldn't be. Fernando was married, I had someone and there were other barriers I was beginning to forget. Everything was new and I floated among the unfamiliar, losing track of my old self.

I can't stop thinking about you. I don't know what to do, he said, in a whisper.

Me too.

He squeezed my hands and I felt his strength running in my blood. It passed my head and limbs, thighs and feet, leaving me empty, erasing the graveyard, the city, turning off the lights. There was nothing besides the wrinkles around his eyes. It was where I wanted to live.

Fernando leaned again and I let him kiss me. One ghostly kiss.

—

We will start with the gypsy deck. This one in the middle is you, José said, placing the tarot cards in the shape of a cross.

José looked like a bull. He was all brown – his skin, eyes and hair, an overlap of earthy tones. The first time I saw him he was wearing colourful rocks around his neck and I had just left work, my dress and cheeks cool from the spring night in São Paulo. His office, in an alternative therapies centre, was painted baby blue and too bright. After walking in the dark, it was comforting to have so much light.

He flipped the first one.

The Tree. It's a good one, he said, smiling.

The Tree represents growing, maturing. An increase in self-knowledge. Six months after I met Fernando, I used to say I felt trapped in a rack, the medieval torture device. There was pain, confusion and a complete ignorance of how it worked – it tore me apart just to pull me closer.

Interesting, José said, turning over the card about my love life. The drawing showed an hourglass with white, black and Asian people inside it.

Past lives.

He stared at me.

Is this the person you are seeing?

I suppose? I mumbled.

Are you together?

Not right now, I mean, I don't think we are.

It's a long story, apparently. Do you think it's over?

No, I don't, I said, keeping my eyes on the glass table, relieved and ashamed.

—

It was raining for the eighth consecutive day when José's voice occupied my bedroom.

The snake, the ring and the lilies, he repeated, his brown face blurry on Skype. I had called him looking for some kind of relief – the water wouldn't stop and I felt I was drowning.

It was a year into our chaos before I travelled to England and Fernando stayed behind. At the airport we cried and made promises, trying to honour the moment. He hit his head with his hands while watching me walk away. It looked like a form of punishment.

This means betrayal, José said slowly, weighing down the words as they came out of his mouth. The snake card represents disloyalty and the lilies and the ring mean union

We would stay together, we swore, just the two of us. But there was always something in the middle. I could never grasp exactly what it was: moral dilemmas, parental loyalty, an emptiness inhabiting one side of my chest while the other built a wall to protect its illusion of wholeness. Fernando wasn't married anymore, he wasn't with me either.

Well… this means betrayal, José said slowly, weighing down the words as they came out of his mouth. The snake card represents disloyalty and the lilies and the ring mean union, usually in a romantic sense.

His hands moved again on the screen, taking one more card against the bright sunlight of São Paulo.

In England, mine were cold.

The Tower, the need to reconstruct your foundations after… sudden changes. This is the deck's advice to you, he added.

I was silent, waiting for the rain to stop.

OK, thank you, I said before disconnecting.

When I called Fernando that night I told him about the predictions and how they concerned me. They covered the three upcoming months, I explained.

Hello, my love, I said. How are you?
On the other end of the line, I heard a heavy sigh.
I can't do this anymore. I'm sorry.

Don't be silly, he said. You're going to become obsessed with these dumb foresights.

I became obsessed by the future in a very subtle way.

When I received his many texts a day, I didn't believe the words. 'Eu te amo', he would write over and over again. 'I love you'. I looked at the phone for a long time before typing: 'Me too'.

Sometimes, we would talk for hours. Other times, I couldn't find the right things to say.

Everything is fine, he assured me one morning, after I woke up from bad dreams. He was in all of them.

A hundred days after my call with José, I was reading Gabriel García Márquez's *The Story of a Shipwrecked Sailor*, the passage where seaman Luis Alejandro Velasco has just given up on life. Starving, he captures a seagull with his hands, wrings its neck, and then perceives that he cannot eat the animal. It is too disgusting. Velasco lies on the raft, having accepted his fate.

My cell phone rang.

Hello, my love, I said. How are you?

On the other end of the line, I heard a heavy sigh.

I can't do this anymore. I'm sorry.

The tenth chapter of *The Story of a Shipwrecked Sailor* is called 'Hope Abandoned … Until Death'. For months its pages remained unread, hidden under the table, thrown there during a conversation I can't completely remember.

I pick up the book to resume the interrupted paragraph. It reads:

'I lay down in the bottom of the raft. I wanted to shout "I'll never get up again," but the words caught in my throat. I remembered school. I raised the Virgin of Carmen medal to my lips and silently began to pray, as I thought my family would be doing just then. Then I felt all right, because I knew I was dying.'[2]

On the next day, the seaman sighted land. ◨

1 J. Woudhuysen, *Tarotmania*, (London, 1979), p.81
2 G.Garcia Marquez, *The Story of a Shipwrecked Sailor*, (London, 1986), p.78

A Week In Churu and Bikaner

by Priya Rajan

Light envelopes the prairie of Tal Chappar blackbuck sanctuary, Churu, Rajasthan well before sunrise, and shines bright for twelve hours in autumn. Twilights splatter hues of pink, orange and russet on the unobscured sky that domes over the plain. At one such sunset, we rode into the sanctuary on a Tonga[1], crossing its half-opened wooden gates. A parakeet above nibbled the shoots of a thorny khejri[2] tree and dropped the stubbles on our heads.

In Western Ghats of southern India, green impersonates blue. Dark green canopy on the distant mountains mirror the blue of the meandering river. In Tal Chappar, green was bathed in yellow. Tufts of tall grass sported sun dried golden brown, mellow yellow and a fickle of green. As the eyes adjusted to the interplay of shades, a few pairs of long, spirally ringed horns rose above the grass towards the sky. Soon, we saw large herds of blackbucks in the grass on either side of the dirt track. While the onyx-backed bucks and the tan-coloured fawns and does grazed unperturbed, the young bachelors, whose backs were darkening from brown to black, lekked restlessly and honed those horns for seasons to come.

Next day, after sunrise, we entered the national park in a jeep with our field guide. A Nilgai[3] who was nursing her calf pricked up her ears to the faint purr of the engine and looked up. After eyeing our distant vehicle for a few seconds, she continued to tend to her calf. Animals here in Tal Chappar are not habituated to human interference. The sanctuary's staff have strived to create and preserve the grassland, which is a homestead to both resident and migratory avifauna. The grassland and the blackbuck population have been revived from decrepitude through decades of conservation efforts; and this small haven thrives amidst the odds that nudge at its boundaries. Persistent Prosopis juliflora trees, an invasive species that has naturalized in the arid regions of India, spread their roots and pods across the fence into the sanctuary, are uprooted and removed by a patrol. This saline depression that receives an annual rainfall of 200mm is a winter haven for many migratory birds.

Ramji, our guide, pointed at a sleek bird of prey that was gliding low and said, 'That is a Montagu harrier. Montagu and Pallid harriers scour low near the grass looking for grasshoppers.' He retrieved a book from the dashboard and showed us the indiscernible differences between the two species. The raptors hovered and circled in the still air for hours, staying close to the unrippled turf, occasionally settling on the dirt to dissect and gobble the insects.

Flocks of demoiselle crane were feeding on seed heads; their slender black necks with bright red eyes and white feathery ear tufts dunking and rising in the thickets of grass. The autumn sun shone strong making us perspire, but the cosmopolitan cranes of Eastern and Central Asia, from the other side of the Himalayas, stayed unperturbed in the fringes of Thar Desert. Unlike us visitors they were at home and had weighed in well. In a fortnight, when the temperature drops in these parts to condense dew on the grass blades, it would already be snowing in Kazakhstan and Mongolia. And, when the temperature soared again in April, coercing the native peacocks to take refuge in the cool, marbled porches of the rest house, the cranes would fly back to their steppes.

A lone tree in the grassland looked distant and timeless. The landscape's solitude seem to converge upon it

A herd of bucks was cooling off at the rim of a pond, and a green sandpiper waded among them looking for insects. The bird must have been named 'green sandpiper' in a similar scene, when the shimmering sunlight evaporated the surface water into a mirage in which the creature's brownish black wings gleamed green. A lone tree in the grassland looked distant and timeless. The landscape's solitude seem to converge upon it. At that moment, we were either nomads in the wilderness of a long gone past, or we dwelt in the expanse of an indefinite future, or both. Nothing broke the spell until a patrolman cycled into the frame and stopped under the tree to take a swig from his water bottle.

'Who comes here in summer?' I asked.

'Birds? People? No one comes here,' said Ramji, 'Loo chalti hain in santal mein.'

'Loo, the heat wave ravages these plains,' he had said. Mouthing the word Loo with caution, letting it out in a whisper as though he could almost see a dust storm rising to cover the sky.

Monsoon winds which bring rains, are much anticipated and celebrated in India, as the country yearns for rain after scorching summer heat. But the pining is nowhere more dramatic than in these western parts of Rajasthan, where the Loo preludes the monsoons, setting the stage. Loo, or Lu, is a hot, dry, dusty summer wind that originates in the north western parts of the Indian sub-continent, and sweeps inwards, browning and burning anything in its path. It is feared and yet revered. Loo shapes the landscape and its culture, music and literature. In an age when bottled water, carton milk and 365-day supermarket vegetables blur the seasons, people etching a living in these arid habitats share a deep connection with their land and the elements.

I pointed at a messy shrub and inquired its name. 'It is Kair[4],' said Ramji.

'Kair? I have heard about Ker-Sangri. Never tasted it,' I said.

'Really? We will make the dish for you before you leave,' said Ramji.

Giridhari, the keeper and the chef of the rest-house had also promised to make the dish when he had showed us a Khejri tree. That afternoon, Ker-Sangri was waiting for us on the lunch table.

Ker-Sangri is a dish made of sour Ker berries and slender sangri bean pods from Kair and Khejri trees. The ripe berries and beans are collected in season, sundried and stored for the rest of the year. The cured vegetables are cooked with generous portions of oil and aromatic spice mix that makes the dish a unique, tangy delicacy. It was either due to the vacation binge or the special mention that I went for multiple helpings of the dish. However, the true flavour of the meal comes from the salt of the earth, its people and their history.

The Khejri tree has cultural, emotional and social significance in the history of Rajasthan. In 1730, the ruler of Marwar[5] ordered his soldiers to collect wood by felling the Khejri trees from the desert village of Khejarli. Amrita Devi Bishnoi[6] and her three daughters offered their heads to be felled instead, to save the trees. Following their example, 363 men, women and children came forward and offered their lives before the massacre was stopped. The act was not rooted in logic but in the spirituality of the Bishnoi community, that believes in the oneness, dignity and equality of all lives.

In the evening, our guide took us to an open land in the village to watch Indian spiny lizards. Switching off the engine, Ramji said, 'Look for plump, dirt-coloured lizards with an exception of blue tail.' For a while I could see nothing. After some direction from Ramji, I spotted a snout at the lip of a burrow and, within seconds, I could see lizards everywhere. Dull brown reptiles neatly camouflaged in dirt, crawling a few metres from their solitary burrows, nibbling, basking in sunlight and scampering at the slightest noise. Suddenly, I saw the barely there blue. A powdery, metal blue speckled on thighs and spikes at the fattened end of the tail. It was like an amateur spotting a constellation in the night sky with field guidance. To spot the blue, the tail had to be mentioned and the lizard had to be at an appropriate angle against the orange sun of the evening sky.

The next day we drove to Bikaner, a desert town, to scale the dunes. The desert of my imagination was that of the Arabian Nights' tales, an uninterrupted rolling expanse of sand marked by golden waves and ochre dunes. But the desert in Bikaner was speckled with sage green, stunted vegetation. Thorny trees obscured the view. We heard piercing calls of francolins from the surrounding shrubs and the wooden wheels of camel carts crunching the sand. However the sunset and the star-studded sky were still as elusive and magical as they are in wonder tales. My three-year-old slid and climbed the dunes more than a dozen times, rolling in the sand.

The desert of my imagination was that of the Arabian Nights' tales, an uninterrupted rolling expanse of sand marked by golden waves and ochre dunes

'She is having all the fun out of Jhor,' said the escort who had driven us to the dunes from our hotel in Bikaner. He used the colloquial word Jhor for dunes, which depicts the rise and fall of a dune in a syllable. He was a wiry man in his early twenties. Unassuming, broad-smiling, with a pair of deep set eyes and crew-cut hair, except for a tiny tuft at the nape.

'It will be a tough time getting the sand out of her locks,' said my husband, pointing at her messy curls.

'At least she is not eating it. We munched the desert sand in our childhood,' said our escort.

According to Indian mythology, there are two ways of seeing the world. One way is to race around the world and the other is to open up to experiences despite staying put. The young man's brush with the wider world happened right in his marusthali[7] region.

Every year, he accompanies doctors ... on an annual journey. They camp, cure and travel through villages by the dirt tracks on camels

'Come winter I go on a medical camp safari through the desert,' he said. Every year, he accompanies surgeons and ophthalmologists from around the world on an annual journey from Bikaner to Pushkar. They camp, cure and travel through villages by the dirt tracks on camels. It is a holiday trip for the specialists, covering 160 miles in 10 days, benefitting the needy along the way.

'I carry the camping essentials and equipment in a jeep,' he said. Reading my mind, he added, 'Though the jeep sounds like an extravagance, it is minimalist living. We slow down, eat what we get and rise and rest with the sun every day.' His narration hushed me; I could not fathom the visions the land revealed to those who made that kind of time and connection.

'It is not in us to open up to uncertainty and

hospitality the way they do,' he said. It was evident that he offered 'us' as a gesture of inclusiveness. He was talking about materialistic people like me, who pack extra pairs in case of rain, carry half the medicine cabinet and a hair dryer for a week's trip.

'My grandfather once went to your city, Bangalore, to work. He made sweets,' he said. 'How apt,' I thought. The traditional sweets and savouries from Bikaner are par excellence; some of the finest brands of Indian confectionary were established by the Halwais (sweet makers) from this region. These entrepreneurs travelled to faraway cities and countries, accompanied by the best hands in the confectionery business. As a non-native friend who lives in Rajasthan says, 'Their sweets ooze two things: ghee and class.'

'Which part of Bangalore did he go to?' I asked.

'I do not know. He returned shortly afterwards and never left. He said the water there didn't suit him.'

Now, that was a statement in contradiction. Though Bangalore of recent years has become an exploding city of dying waterbodies, unlike in the sandy and arid Bikaner, the monsoon winds come into the city in the month of June and drench it for the next five months. Swollen clouds that resemble a confectioner's luscious sweets, loom large and douse the scorching summer. Yet, a man from these hot plains did not find solace in that climate. The juxtaposition stayed in my mind for days.

Over the next few days, we drove through a landscape that glimmered in the autumn sun, our eyes meeting horizon on all sides. Men and women toiled on spotty patches of green at the fringes of the desert. Pink of the women's skirts and yellow and amber of the herdsmen's headgear dotted the bronzed earth and the azure sky.

On a lull afternoon, gazing from the backseat, I realized that the sweet-maker would have gone from here to the crowded streets of a booming city. There, nights often ambushed from the obscured skies, and the dusks that unfurl through layers of pink, orange and amber go unheeded. I wondered if the city's tongue had startled him in the beginning. Because it was not only alien, but also a hurried one which rushed and crushed its diphthongs and syllables. Much like the concreted city walkways that are isolated from the soil crushed underneath.

Would he have yearned for his parched land and its lingo when the rains pattered on his roof? As quoted by eminent environmentalist Anupam Mishra in his book[8]: [It is]a dialect in which the names of clouds literally seem to overcast the sky. The nomenclature for clouds is so vast that clouds might fall short of them.

As we left for the airport, I wondered if the confectioner longed for these hot plains and its hovering sky and tried to pithily sum up that inexplicable ache as 'the water did not suit him.' **H**

1.Tonga: A one-horse carriage.
2. Khejri: A thorny tree native to the Indian Subcontinent and Western Asia; the state tree of Rajasthan.
3. Nilgai: Largest Asian antelope, whose name means 'blue cow'.
4. Kair: A shrub native to arid regions of southern Asia, Africa and the Middle East.
5. Marwar: A region in South Western Rajasthan near Thar Desert.
6. The legend of Amrita Devi and environmentalism of Bhishnois can be found in various books and websites, including Wikipedia.
7. Marusthali: The north western region of Rajasthan comprising of Thar, Great Indian Desert, and the arid regions surrounding it.
8. From the book Radiant drops of Rajasthan by Anupam Mishra, translated by Maya Jani. Original Hindi text is titled, Rajasthan ki rajat boonde.

Double page
spread,
full colour –
£350

Single page,
full colour –
£200

Half page,
full colour –
£120

Single page,
b&w – £150

Half page,
b&w – £70

HINTERLAND

Hinterland publishes the bestselling
authors you know and love, as well as
the fresh new voices of tomorrow.
Our readers are intelligent,
creative and curious.
If this is the company you'd like
to keep, consider advertising
your product or service with us.

IN CONVERSATION WITH
Tessa McWatt

*Hinterland editor Andrew Kenrick and contributing editor
Yin F. Lim sat down with Tessa McWatt, author and
Professor of Creative Writing at the University of East
Anglia, to discuss her memoir* Shame On Me, *in a
conversation which delved into racism and antiracism,
the Meghan Markle effect, and the relationship between
literature and activism.*

Yin F. Lim: I just finished *Shame On Me* and given
what's been in the news these past few weeks, I got
goosebumps.

Tessa McWatt: It is timely, isn't it?

Andrew Kenrick: Just in the weeks since we spoke
to you [about doing an interview] and certainly
since I started reading the book there's been the
Meghan Markle story, and questions about white
privilege on the BBC's *Question Time*.

TM: What's really disturbing and interesting is
that it's been timely for people of colour forever. It's
only considered timely now because there are other
[white] people being pushed back. So the pressure
to recognise that racism is a huge issue consciously
and unconsciously is [phew] right there, right in
front of us.

AK: So you're saying that now it's beginning to intrude on the consciousness of the wider public?

TM: There are other forces that are making it a perfect storm; the press, the Meghan Markle stuff, Brexit, all kinds of things going on in the States. One of the reasons why I wrote this book was because, in 2016, my dad died, then there was Brexit and then the US election. I just thought there is such a division here and I need to state my case, which is kind of a bridging case. But I don't know if it serves people who have always experienced anti-black racism. They go 'yeh, yeh, I know, that's what we've been experiencing' but it does serve people who haven't thought about it.

YL: When we first met at the UEA literary festival, I remember you said 'I am now angry enough to write my memoir.'

TM: Oh really?

YL: Yes, that's always stuck with me. Especially reading this now, I understand the anger better. Was there a catalyst or turning point where any reservations you had about putting yourself out there diminished?

TM: Even now I have reservations about having written it, because anything you write is on the page and it belongs to a moment, it's not necessarily how you're feeling now. So there's a bit of reservation thinking 'what was that moment?' It's stayed the same, I'm still as angry, I'm still as upset, I'm still watching the argument, the black and the white for want of better words, are still clashing and making me uncomfortable. So it's the discomfort, as well as the anger. The anger I could probably take out by involvement in politics or sitting in the street for Extinction Rebellion – all of which I do – but it's that discomfort, trying to pin down the fine points rather than the sound bites, trying to pinpoint the subtleties of this, the micro-aggressions, the unawareness, the subtleties of being slightly asleep to what's going on around you, but from many directions.

YL: Is that what you hope your book contributes to the whole conversation?

TM: I do. I hope it picks apart some of the black and white. That it nuances and makes it more complicated than that. Because one of the points I make in the book is that the 'plantation owners,' as I call them, love it when we fight. They love it when it's black vs. white, because they can go on to run their plantations and make their profits while we're fighting against each other on the plantation. So the book is about pointing at where the real problems are.

YL: It's about opening up conversations – it's not as simple as saying 'this is racism' or 'that's racism'.

TM: It's not a question of whether racism exists or not: it does. And it's not a question of whether

Britain is a racist country: it is. It's just how does it manifest itself and how is it systemic and how is it other things? How is it part of being British, how is it part of the structure and how does it cause people to behave in reaction to a given moment?

AK: And whenever those sorts of conversations occur, the mainstream media seems to deal with it very superficially. I'm thinking of when Stormzy was asked whether Britain was still racist – his comments were misrepresented , and the conversation became 'Stormzy says Britain's a racist country, how dare he say it's a racist country'. It all becomes reduced to fighting over the surface details without really engaging in the conversation.

TM: Yes, absolutely. And to not even be able to acknowledge that I've had this experience. You can't tell me that it's not racism if it's my experience. You can't deny my experience, because that's the ultimate in white supremacy, right: 'you didn't have that experience, that doesn't happen.'

YL: It's like gaslighting, isn't it?

TM: Completely.

YL: Because the more you go on about how you got it wrong, the more...

TM: ... it becomes my fault. I was wrong. I'm misinterpreting. I'm oversensitive. I'm just a victim.

And that's why, in the book, I use scare quotes
– 'black', 'white', 'yellow', 'brown' – as a way of
highlighting the way that language is a tool, but
also a weapon, and that we need to be very careful
of it. We're all products of language, we're all built
on stories. And we need to be careful about the
stories we tell and how we hear them. We now have
a whole bunch of new stories about race – we have
Meghan Markle, we have Lawrence Fox, they're
stories – and how we hold those stories and how
we tell them and how we interpret them are really
important to a contemporary way of understanding
what we're doing as 'othering' people.

AK: When you're discussing – or teaching – history,
it can be dangerous to project modern views and
language on the past. There are nuances in there
we're not always aware of. But there are people who
want to whitewash our view of the past, for their
own modern agenda.

TM: I guess I was trying to find out why we need
to draw boundaries that keep us tribal, that keep us
white, black, keep that purity, keep that tribe safe.
There are threats from the 'outside'. Why do we
have those threats? Because in my interpretation
of it, capitalism tells us there's a threat because
we're in competition with each other and if we're in
competition with each other there's not enough. It
says that 'I don't have enough and therefore I need
to keep you out' and so you become other. And if
you are from the power base, that usually comes

swiftly and brutally. No matter what the current other is, there's always an 'other'; currently in the West it's probably Muslims. Throughout our history there's always been a reason to put that border up, and borders are the essence of racism. I saw this photo that went viral on social media recently, of a Joey – a baby kangaroo – stuck in a fence, burnt and charred during the Australian bush fires. But it was the detail of the fence that was so awful, because the kangaroo was running away and it got stuck in the fence and died; it made my heart race and my blood churn. And there's so much about that that's absolutely wrong: people – creatures – fleeing who can't get to where they want to go because of that border, and that border defines others. Others can't get into our space. And I think we have to examine why we need that border.

AK: What's the reaction been to the book?

TM: Oh it's been really good, on an individual level. I've had amazing responses, from lots of different kinds of people, but mostly from people of mixed race who say 'I've never seen myself in a book, ever, until now.' This 35-year-old woman wrote to me and said 'no one has ever written about me before', so that's really lovely. A lot of people who say 'I've never looked at myself, looked at race, at whiteness as a state of mind' before.

AK: I have a question about intimacy, and this is a question that we often ask authors of memoir and autobiography: having read it I feel like I know you, know a different side of you. What's the reaction of friends and family been in that regard?

TM: My family's all fine with it. My friends who are not necessarily intimates say 'I never knew that, I never knew that was how you were experiencing the world.' They're surprised, and a little bit blocked out of those things. And it's true, I don't wear those reactions in my everyday life – I mean, I fight for those issues, but I don't wear them all the time. Essentially, I'm a privileged person, so I don't walk around reacting to things if they're about me. I do if they're about other people and power dynamics that hurt them.

YL: That's an interesting point about privilege. I was talking [to Andrew] about this conversation I had about Afua Hirsch's book, *Brit-ish*. Well, the other person said 'it's quite a strident voice… and she's privileged.' Almost as if because she's from a privileged background she's got no right to talk about race. I felt that's all the more reason you do.

TM: It's why I wrote this particular book and not any other book about race. The shame is on me, as well as on other privileged people. The shame is on me because of the whiteness, because of privilege and liberalism and how 'attainment' can be seen to be outside of race, to be post-racial. But the world is not post-racial. I happen to work in the master's house and not in the field. That's all that means.

And the book is a lot about me recognising that, and that's where the privilege is.

YL: Your book ends with hope, and I wondered: does that hope extend to dismantling the master's house? You touch on the next generation.

TM: Not just the next generation. Now, with the burning, flooding, decimated planet, we could say 'Stop! Let's look at what we're doing.' The planet needs us to stop and look at each other and say 'we need to do something together here.' I'm not that hopeful. I'm hopeful in that I think individuals can ask 'who am I?' And then they can join together and have better conversations, but I'm not 100% convinced that we're not on some kind of self-destruct path. I don't think I would have said that when I finished writing the book, but maybe we've gone too far since then.

AK: Because we've had three years of this country tearing itself apart, and we've just doubled down by electing a Conservative majority.

TM: We've doubled down. And I think had I written the book after the election I might have been less optimistic. I don't know. I think there is a place for slow, individual change and for those individuals to join up and form groups. For me, if I don't resist and push back against what's going on now, I don't want to be here. So I have to push back. And maybe if everyone who feels that joins together… But I'm less confident that we can really change anything soon. Maybe it's over the long haul – but the really long haul.

AK: Those mass protest movements like Extinction Rebellion seemed to have captured the imagination last year – but are they having an impact?

TM: I'm not sure. I just came back from Barbados at Christmas; I have family there. But I was surprised by how much blind consumption through tourism still thrives. Fiddling while Rome burns. I don't want to say that I'm not hopeful, because the book does end with hope, but… I need to find it again. I need to find that hope again.

YL: After the Brexit referendum there was a point that I thought 'at least people are having the conversation.' Before that they weren't, people were very much 'oh no, it doesn't exist, we're very open minded here.' But I think after Brexit people started talking about it. If there's any plus point about any of these horrible things it's that new people are coming forward with their own voices; they're not holding back any more; they've got a say in this.

TM: I agree, but it just feels that the voices are more polarised. That it's gone back to a lot of hate. After the 2019 election I thought 'OK, you don't want me here, I'll leave,' because that's what the massive support for a Tory Brexit felt like. And I feel a lot more resigned than I ever have before. [Pause]

Gosh, this is terrible. I'm really glad you picked up on the hope in the book, because that's what I wanted there to be.

AK: Did you decide to write a book about race or did you decide to write a memoir, or were they always connected?

TM: They were always connected. I'd always had the idea that I'd break it down, break the race discussion down into body parts. And so then as soon as I decided that I thought I can't only objectify the body because that's what other people do; I wanted to undermine race and take it on at the same time. I wanted to be responsible, because I cannot speak for everyone, I can only speak for myself, that complicated self; and in speaking for that complicated self, it's a complicated argument. So in a way it was a book I was born to write. Nobody else – that I know – could have done it that way, and I had to do it at that moment.

AK: That's interesting to hear about the decision to structure the book around the body, because we were wondering if that came later in the process, but it sounds like it was very much there from the start.

TM: That was at the very beginning. Because I don't fulfil the quintessential body types of any those so-called races, I had to break it down that way.

YL: So it became an interrogation.

TM: Yeh.

YL: I thought it was interesting that you took an almost scientific approach.

TM: It very much is an experiment in many ways. It's an experiment in non-fiction, and it's an experiment in a discussion about an essay vs. a memoir. It's a hybrid, like me.

YL: When you're dealing with family history, when you're writing about yourself, it's often based on memory. In particular with family history, you never get everything, do you? I was wondering whether hybridity was the solution to dealing with those gaps?

TM: Absolutely. I fictionalise some of my ancestors because I don't have access to them. Hybridity of form, hybridity of approach, hybridity of the physicality of things. I think that's probably the organising principle behind the book.

AK: Did you find that challenging? There's a tendency when writing non-fiction to smooth the story, especially when you've come from a fiction background where all the answers for the story are within you. Did you find...

TM: ...being constrained by truth a problem? Yes! It's not so much that the truth was a problem. I'm a storyteller, and so it was telling a real story. I think everybody is a storyteller, even science is storytelling on many levels. If you want to expose a truth, you tell a story around it, whether it's setting up petri dishes to confirm that story or narrating it. I think science and literature, science and art, have a lot more in common than scientists allow for. I recently talked to Christie Watson, author of *The Language of Kindness* and someone who is steeped in medical humanities, and told her what I do – not for this book, but I have another project that's mentioned in the book, my loneliness project. I said 'we share stories against loneliness,' and she said 'that's medicine.' Storytelling is what medicine needs, and that's one of Christie's points, that patients need to be able to tell their stories in order to get well.

AK: I was going to ask you about shifting from writing fiction to non-fiction, but it sounds like it wasn't so much of a shift.

TM: Not so much. I had written the draft of a novel before I wrote this, then I won the Eccles British Library award for *Shame On Me* and my agent sold it, so then I had to get it finished. I've since gone back to the novel and have just handed it in to my agent. It was a joy to go back to in many ways; because you don't have to worry about the truth. But my next book is non-fiction, so...

AK: Do you think some of the themes that you touch upon in this book, that you've uncovered, will reoccur in your fiction?

TM: You'll see them if you read my next novel, which is a kind of King Lear for brown girls. It's about that dying off of that superior, white narrative; it's got an older man, an 86-year-old man, and a young Indian woman, who's a Cordelia figure for him. And so those themes are definitely there. Power dynamics are in almost everything I've written.

YL: There was something that struck me when I read the acknowledgements in the book, where you thanked your publisher for encouraging you not to hide behind your ideas.

TM: Yes, she really challenged me. Because I had used all sorts of passive constructions, my sentences had a fairly academic tone, and she asked where I was in all of this. She made me come out from behind that style of quite formal language and into the forefront of the writing, so that it became much more 'I' centred.

YL: How did that feel? Because this is really personal, that must have been very uncomfortable.

TM: It was at first, but she coaxed it gently. The things that I exposed were always going to be the same, but it's the way the sentences were constructed that changed and became more personal. And so it probably felt more personal to you as a result, but to me it was always that same amount of exposure but I was hiding behind that language of essay-writing, rather than using a more confessional tone.

AK: That's bold and brave, to inhabit the book so fully there's no shield to hide behind.

TM: There's authority in that as well. I knew when I was writing it everything had to come back to me, because I didn't want to make big statements about things I didn't know about. I don't know about other people's experiences, so I had to make them about me. So the personal was always going to be the political. That's the only way I could justify the political, by making it personal.

YL: And the authority from which you speak was the personal.

AK: What were some of the other challenges you faced when writing this? Because one of the problems about writing family history is that, by its very nature, it relies upon certain members of the family, some of it's locked away from you. When writing 'real' history, you can go to archives, you can look it up, but with family history it's personal. That sort of history isn't in a book.

TM: Most of it is oral history, most of it is family stories. And most of the stories were reliant upon my mother, who's got dementia! Her dementia was just beginning when I wrote it, but she doesn't remember some of the things she told me. So it became, again, a question of: how do you know what's true, how do you know what's real? And history books are one kind of authority, but is that book authority – is what someone said about race back in the seventeenth, eighteenth century – any more authoritative than my ancestors' stories? No, because since then we've challenged those authorities. Storytelling on the level of race science is still very much storytelling.

YL: So you can't treat all authorities, all stories, the same.

TM: No, how can you? Or else you'd believe those race superiority stories, you'd believe Africans were inferior, if you believed all science at all times.

YL: Your mother is a central character in the book, and your grandmother. There's obviously a very strong bond there. Did your stories mainly come from them?

TM: From family, yes. From my cousin, who lives in London and who's got a memory like a steel trap. He's 6 or 7 years older than me and lived in Guyana longer so he has a better memory of it. So a lot of the research was relying on everybody else's stories, as well as a bit of research on the McWatt family tree. That's how I know my great-great-grandfather came from East Lothian, but why what happened in Guyana, and who got his name and who didn't get his name, is the unknown. A lot of those are hush-hush family secrets.

AK: In the book you encounter this other McWatt...

TM: ... the big black Dr McWatt. Which was an incredible moment, when I saw my dad's name – because he was also Dr McWatt – on the oxygen cylinder at the airport. And my dad had just died, needing oxygen.

AK: Did you ever find where your families intersected?

TM: Yes, my great-great-grandfather's cousin was his line of the family.

AK: There's that pressure in recovering the stories. I got very interested in my family history when my mum died, because she was the custodian of the family story and I felt this real drive to go and see my grandad, who was very old at the time, and to talk to him and get these stories out of him. There was that need to find out, and that regret for not finding out sooner.

TM: Do you feel regret?

AK: Yes, in some respect.

TM: And you feel, how am I going to know? You might have to write fiction now to fill in the gaps [laughs].

YL: I was thinking about the importance of stories from women, because you talk about suppressed voices. So, in a way, bringing stories from your mother and grandmother is a way of giving them a voice.

TM: And I can trace the McWatt side, but I can't trace my mother's side except through her father, so that female lineage is always blocked by the name change, and denied. And because, in this case, nobody in my family acknowledged my great-great-African grandmother. I don't know where she sits. I asked my cousin about her, because they knew her son, but they don't know. Nobody knows anything about her.

AK: Were there any other spurs of your family that you were interested in, but you couldn't get to?

TM: I was really close to my Chinese grandmother, so I'd really like to find out more about her family. And then there's the Amerindian side.

AK: Which is where you had to fictionalise your ancestor?

TM: Yeh. As a Canadian, the indigenous issue is very important. It's one thing to have bloodlines, it's another thing to claim an identity that you have no experience of. And that's where cultural appropriation comes into play. It would be great if we were all trans-racial, but that doesn't speak to people's experiences. Because it's often not about skin colour, it's about experiences, it's about poverty, it's about violence. And sometimes those experiences have nothing to do with race – it goes along with race, because we're on the plantation, but not always.

AK: You mentioned earlier about the need of a capitalist society to 'other' certain people, and at times that's been a class rather than race-based othering.

TM: It still very much is class othering, especially in this country. I'm such a naïve North American. I came over thinking it would just go away, it would get better, because there's a kind of meritocracy in North America that just doesn't seem to exist here. And I think I've only realised that in the last 5 years, and I've been here for 21 years. Meghan Markle has made the first good move, she's started to dismantle the royalty, but it's not going to be enough.

AK: And the press' response to that, the outcry...

TM: 'How dare she? She's ruined him. This uppity black woman has taken away our prince. Ruined the monarchy.' Good on her. I wasn't a big fan of her before, I couldn't care less about her, but I like her more now. But there's something very elemental about the British Empire, in this country. I don't know if it will go away.

AK: A lot of the arguments supporting Brexit revolved around sovereignty and a return to a 'golden age' that probably never existed...

TM: Or existed on the backs of those other people that they didn't know about, who were harvesting their sugar.

YL: That they chose not to see.

TM: How are you, Andrew, where do you sit? What do you feel about all of this?

AK: Very uncomfortable. I'm a staunch Remain voter, but before that I admit that I thought all of these problems had been fixed. I couldn't see the problem. I come at it from a slightly different angle, because I'm gay. I came out in my thirties, and I freely admit my experiences as a white middle-class man coming out in the noughties would have been a very different experience from a working-class or black man coming out, or someone coming out in the eighties or nineties.

TM: So you have a sense of where you sit relative to the othering.

AK: And I'm keenly aware of my own privilege because of that. Which is why I'm very careful when we have these sorts of conversations, although I like to think that I'm aware of that privilege that I've enjoyed. Because my coming out story was very boring: I told my mum I was gay and everyone accepted me, the end. I don't want to project my experiences onto questions of race, though. But that does then make me feel like I don't own the identity; because I've never felt that pressure, I've never felt that victimhood. I've never felt that homophobia.

TM: But that's exactly what the book asks you: who are you relative to inequalities? I don't know if you've heard of Ibram Kendi's book *How to be an Antiracist,* in which he says there's no such thing as being not racist – we're all racist. The difference is are you antiracist, do you have antiracist actions. I wrote a TLS review that doesn't speak well of the book necessarily, but this one thing is very clear, it's not about doing nothing, it's not about saying 'I'm not a racist so I don't need to do anything.' It's about where are you when that's in your face, and how antiracist are you. It's a really good marker. You might be privileged and you might be all kinds of things but in the face of homophobia and racism, who are you, what do you do? And I think that's a good marker, that action, verbal as well as physical action. Who are you in the face of climate collapse, who are you in the face of racism?

AK: Are you a bystander, in which case you're complicit.

YL: I was going to ask you about action. Do you think that's the path you'll take going forwards?

TM: Yes, writing is one thing, but not every book hits a mark with other people. Writing is action, it's definitely important, but writing is aimed at people who read. And at people who read a certain kind – a certain level – of writing, so it's not enough to just write. Especially with the climate crisis, it's not enough. When the book came out [in October

2019], I went from recording Start the Week with Lenny Henry, Keon West and Matthew Syed on Radio 4, to sitting and blocking a road in Trafalgar Square, because it was the same day as the last Extinction Rebellion action started. So that felt good; I went from saying stuff to blockading the road. I was accompanied by people who felt the same. To do something, and to do something with other people, feels good.

Shame On Me is out now in hardback from Scribe. ⬛

Like what you've read?

Look out for the fifth issue of Hinterland, on sale June 2020. Better still, sign up for a subscription and get our next batch of stand-out writing delivered direct to your door, desktop or tablet.

Annual print & digital subscription £34
Four issues, saving £6 off list price

Annual digital subscription £20
Four issues, saving £4 off list price

Subscribers also enjoy the benefit of being able to submit their writing to Hinterland free of charge.

Visit our website to subscribe:

www.hinterlandnonfiction.com/subscribe